IN SOFT GARMENTS

Uniform with this volume

THE HIDDEN STREAM
(A further Collection of Oxford Conferences)

IN SOFT GARMENTS

A Collection of
Oxford Conferences

by

RONALD A. KNOX

They that are clothed in soft garments are
in the Palaces of Kings.—*Matthew* xi. 8.

NEW YORK

SHEED AND WARD INC.

1958

NIHIL OBSTAT: THOMAS E. BIRD, S.T.D.

CENSOR DEPVTATVS

IMPRIMATVR: ✠ THOMAS

ARCHIEPISCOPVS BIRMINGAMIENSIS

BIRMINGAMIAE: DIE VIII NOVEMBRIS MCMXLI

First published Jan. 1942

Reprinted Sept. 1942

Second edition 1953

Reprinted 1958

PRINTED IN GREAT BRITAIN.

To

GERVASE MATHEW

of the Order of Preachers,

for whom this book contains nothing new.

PREFACE

WHEN the Holy See gave a general permission for Catholics to matriculate at Oxford and Cambridge, the stipulation was made that lectures should be provided for them, to safeguard their faith against the influence of an uncongenial atmosphere. During the years between 1926 and 1938, when I was chaplain at Oxford, I delivered a good many of these myself; and I have collected some of them in this book, in the hope that they may suggest useful lines of thought to a wider (though I hope not much more learned) audience. In particular, I suppose that the subjects here discussed are such as figure, not infrequently, in the programme of the Catholic Evidence Guild. It will be seen, from a glance at the title-page, that this book does not represent a complete course in any branch of apologetics. But I have tried to deal, unprofessionally, with some of the hesitations that most naturally occur to us Catholics, when we compare our intellectual commitments with the current thought of the present day. I have only altered the text where it contained topical allusions which might baffle the uninitiated reader. If I have not gone further, by removing traces of colloquialism and undignified illustrations here and there, it is because I dare to hope some of those who listened to the original utterances will come across the book (in circumstances how strangely remote from the past!), and refresh themselves, as they turn over its pages, with the memory of familiar things.

R. A. KNOX

Aldenham, 1941.

CONTENTS

THE CROSS-WORD OF CREATION

THE fifth of the five classical arguments for the existence of God is taken from the existence of order in the natural world, and infers from that the existence of an eternal Mind which devised it. That is, on the whole, the stupid man's argument, which makes it convenient for me to treat of it; also it is the argument which is most discussed nowadays, partly for the same reason, and partly because the scientific materialists are always discovering, every fifty years or so, that they have now found out a way of giving it its deathblow. Let me just state it first of all as St Thomas gives it. "We see that some things, which lack consciousness, namely natural bodies, work for an end; which appears from the fact that they work always or quite frequently in a uniform way, so as to achieve that which is best. Whence it is clear that they reach their end not by mere chance but by intention. But things which have no consciousness do not aim at an end unless they are directed by some one who has consciousness and intelligence, as an arrow is directed by the archer. Therefore there is some intelligent principle by which natural things are ordained to an end; and this we call God."

Now, that is really an argument from the existence of order or law in nature generally; it is not simply the popular argument from design. The argument from *design* is an attempt to prove the existence of God and the Goodness of God in one.

It says, How could such and such things happen unless a fatherly Providence had arranged that they should happen? For example, about this time of the year you get those red berries on the hedges which I used to call hips and haws. And it was a belief instilled into my childhood that if you found a great many of them on the hedges in autumn it meant there was going to be a very cold winter. The ground would be so hard or so covered in snow that the poor little dicky-birds wouldn't be able to get any nice worms to eat, so Providence had arranged that they should have berries instead. I have never been able to persuade myself that the facts were as stated; but if they are it is easy to see the force of the argument. "It can't be just an accident that the berries are always there in abundance just when they are most wanted; you can only explain it by supposing that there is a beneficent Mind at work conspiring for the conservation of creatures."

Of course that nursery argument gets more difficult when you are outside the nursery. It involves the assumption that you know what is best, and believe in God because you find him doing it. We saw our aunts throwing bread-crumbs out of the front window, and we pictured Providence as throwing hips and haws out of the front windows of heaven to secure the same self-evidently good end—namely the survival of the dicky-birds. It was only later we came to realize that if no birds were killed off by frosts, cats, and other natural means, the world would become uncomfortably crowded with birds and there would be less fruit in the garden. And that is, of course, the bother about the argument from design; you are up against the pessimist who says, "Yes, but I can't see that what you call Providence *is* working to a good end." As Lord Russell puts it with his usual trenchancy, "Do you think that, if you were granted omnipotence and omniscience and millions of years in which to perfect your world, you could produce nothing better than Ku Klux Klan and the Fascisti and Mr Winston Churchill?'' The bother is we don't understand what God's plan is; we aren't meant to; we are only meant to see it in bits. And to that extent any argument based on the beneficence of Providence is difficult to bring home to people. But, of course, what has killed the argument from design from the man in the street's point of view—and in such matters the man in the street does not greatly differ from the man in the quad—is the Darwinian theory of natural selection. We used to think how kind it was of Providence to have given the Polar bear a nice woolly coat before putting it down in the Arctic regions. The chimpanzee, for example, which has a delicate chest, would never have stood the rigours of an Arctic winter. Well, since Darwin popularized natural selection, we have a different explanation of all that. Either the Polar bear trekked northwards to find food, not minding the cold, whereas the chimpanzee stayed at home; or else there were originally chimpanzees at the North Pole, but later it turned cold there and killed off the chimpanzees while leaving the Polar bears. There's no design about it; only just accident.

Well, of course, we all know that the last word hasn't been said yet about the doctrine of natural selection. One thing is quite clear, and that is that it doesn't explain all that it set out to explain; the scientists have quite given up supposing that it can. But the man in the street, and with him the man in the quad, have come to take this rather dated point of view so much for granted, that it is no longer any use talking to them about design. So what I want to put before you this morning is the argument from order and law in nature. And I don't believe that St Thomas meant to use the argument from design when he gave his fifth proof. I don't think what impressed St Thomas was the fact that everything conspires together for a beneficent purpose; what impressed him was the fact that things conspire together at all. "We see things," he says, "of different natures agreeing in one order, not occasionally or as if by chance, but always or in the greater number of instances." We are not concerned to prove that the world was ordained by a loving Mind; all we are out to prove is that, for better or worse, it was ordained by a Mind, and there is no other explanation of it.

To see that argument in its crude form you have only to isolate some corner of nature as we know it, and reflect on the order which we observe there. We won't talk about sunsets or the song of the nightingale, we won't bring sentiment into the thing at all. But take, say, the geometrical patterns which frost makes on a window-pane. A pattern, repeated again and again; a pattern, based on certain mathematical proportions; how did that get there? If you tried drawing those same patterns with your eyes shut, how often would you get them right? And if mere naked chance ruled the universe, why should nature produce patterns any more than you would drawing with your eyes shut? The delicate tracery of a leaf, the exact design into which sand falls on a brass plate, when a violin-bow is drawn along the edge—how is it, unless there is a Mind to direct them, that inanimate things work themselves out according to a fixed scheme, not occasionally or as if by chance, but always or in the great majority of instances? Why, inanimate nature can actually beat our intelligent minds when it comes to putting the scheme into practice. We have in our heads the idea of a straight line, but we can't *draw* a straight line. If you put a blade of grass and a razor blade under a microscope, the grass is really a straight line, and the razor is all waggly. Order, then, in nature, is something which our minds can appreciate; but our minds didn't put it there; our minds find it there. And what put it there, except another Mind? A cross-word which a mind can solve took a mind to make it up. Order is the cipher by which Mind speaks to mind in the midst of chaos; that's what we mean by the fifth proof.

In order to appreciate the strength of that argument, it is instructive to notice how the more intelligent opponents of Christianity labour to destroy it, and how ineffectively. Lord Russell, for example, in his tract called *Why I am not a Christian*, actually tries to play off against us the principle of indeterminacy. He says: "Where you can actually get down to any knowledge of what atoms actually do, you find that they are much less subject to law than people thought, and that the laws at which you arrive are statistical averages of just the sort that would emerge from mere chance. . . . That makes this whole business of natural law much less impressive than it formerly was." He refers, of course, to all that Heisenberg business which was popularized by Sir James Jeans some years ago; the idea that when you get down to the tiniest components of the atom you find that they don't work, apparently, by any law; they each act as they choose, so to speak, and it is only the law of averages that puts things right. Very well then, says Lord Russell, where's your law and order in nature now? It's all anarchy, governed by statistics. That was some years ago; since then, Sir Arthur Eddington has been exploiting this same principle of indeterminacy in the interests of religion; he uses it, for example, to defend free will. Accordingly you find Lord Russell in his book, *The Scientific Outlook*, arguing feverishly on exactly the opposite side. "The principle of Indeterminacy does nothing whatever to show that the course of nature is not determined. . . . The principle of Indeterminacy has to do with measurement, not with causation. . . . There is nothing whatever in the principle of Indeterminacy to show that any physical event is uncaused." Just so; I have no doubt he is quite right; the fact that we cannot predict the behaviour of the atom does not mean that the behaviour of the atom is arbitrary. Only, what a pity Lord

Russell did not remember that in the Battersea Town Hall, on Sunday, March 6, 1927, at a meeting summoned under the auspices of the South London branch of the National Secular Society, he himself used this same principle of indeterminacy to show that the argument from order in nature was no longer any use!

I always find it so hard to imagine how people can look at the order of creation around them and content their minds with the supposition that it got there by chance. Nothing but dead matter to start with, and then mysteriously arising amidst that dead matter living things, with the power of organic growth; and then amidst those living things, mysteriously again, conscious things, capable of feeling and of moving from place to place; and then amidst those conscious things, still more mysteriously, a self-conscious being, Man, with his mind capable of turning back upon itself and becoming its own object. The whole of creation leading up gradually to higher and higher stages of existence, with Mind as the last stage of all—and yet somehow Mind must have been there from the first, or how, from the first, did cosmos emerge from chaos; how, from the first, could creation have contained the germs of Mind, unless Mind had put them there? What do they make of it all, the materialists?

Oh, they say, that's all right; it's just a sort of accident, a sort of outside chance; after all, sooner or later these outside chances are bound to come off. Look at all the millions of worlds there are; is it very surprising that just a few of them, perhaps two or three, should have had the kind of climate which makes life possible? And since that happened, it was more or less bound to happen that in one of these at least the possibility should be actually realized, and life, followed by conscious life, followed by self-conscious life, should appear. I've never been able to find that argument very impressive;

it starts all right, but it seems to flicker in the middle. I mean, it's quite easy to see that with millions of worlds about you are likely to get one or two, and one or two only, with the kind of climate we have, on which, therefore, life is possible. But it's one thing to say the odds are on there being one or two bodies, like Mars and ourselves, on which life is *possible*; it's quite another thing to say the odds are on life actually *coming to exist*, here or in Mars or anywhere. As I wrote in a book somewhere, "if the police were to discover a human body in Lord Russell's Saratoga trunk, he would not be able to satisfy them with the explanation that, among all the innumerable articles of luggage in the world, it is only natural that there should be some few which are large enough to contain a body. They would want to know how it got there." How did life arise—just out of a particular lot of atoms happening to get jumbled together? If so, there is our second coincidence; those particular atoms happen to get jumbled up on a planet with a climate which happens to support life; and that life happens to survive. And later on, by a fresh accident, some of these plants happen to develop sensation, and these sensitive plants happen to survive and become animals; and then certain animals happen to develop the habit of reflective thought, and those particular animals happen to survive, and turn into men—altogether there is rather too much coincidence there. Accident is all right as an explanation at first, but there comes a point at which the thing begins to look like carelessness.

And, of course, even if you could prove that life (for example) arises automatically out of some particular arrangement of atoms—we haven't proved it, and we are no nearer proving it than we ever were—the question would still remain to be asked, what power it was which ordained that such an arrangement of atoms should result in the birth of a quite new order of existence; "that out of three sounds he frame, not a fourth sound, but a star." It's no good telling us that the forces of nature did that; nature is only an abstraction, and the forces of nature are only abstractions; abstractions can't impose their will on real things. You must believe, sooner or later, in a Mind which brought mind into existence out of matter, unless you are going to sit down before the hopeless metaphysical contradiction of saying that matter somehow managed to develop itself into mind.

I'm afraid I've wandered about a good deal, and perhaps tried to take in too much in my argument. But I did want you to see that the argument from order in the universe is not, necessarily at any rate, the same as the argument from design. It's not necessary for us to prove that we are living in the best of all possible worlds; it doesn't matter (for the purposes of our present argument) whether the laws we find in nature are beneficent or harmful in their operation; the point is that order exists in the Universe, and that it is logically impossible to conceive of order existing without a Mind. And if we denied the existence of that Mind, and went on thinking about it hard, it wouldn't be very long, I fancy, before most of us would go out of our own.

II

"MIND" AND "MATTER"

WHEN I talk about mind and matter, I am not going to attempt any precise definition of those terms; I am going to use them in a popular sense, the good, old-fashioned sense in which they were used by late-Victorian journalists. In that loose sense, the two terms between them exhaust our experience; everything of which we are conscious falls under one head or the other. Matter stands for all those things other than oneself, outside oneself (if I may use such grossly popular terms), which form the object of one's experience; it is the brute fact which you can't get away from, the rude reality which obtrudes itself into your thought. If you are in the dentist's chair and shut your eyes and try to imagine that you are in a hot bath or in a punt on the river, that relentless drill comes buzzing round and having fun with your nerves, the symbol of matter triumphing over mind, insisting on making itself felt and being taken into consideration. The pleasant kingdom of the mind has no real frontiers to defend it; our thought cannot just select its own objects, as it would like to, they force themselves upon it; there is a something not ourselves which we cannot control or organize at will; let that serve for our very inadequate definition of matter.

But matter doesn't cover the whole of our experience; there can be no experience unless there is a mind to do the

9

experiencing. If you tell a man to count how many people there are in the room, the odds are that he will return the figure one short, because by a trick of unconscious modesty he will have forgotten to include himself. And in the same sort of way unreflective people will be so absorbed in the things which are the objects of their experience, that they will forget the part which their mind plays in it all. I remember long ago, when he was a young don, the present Archbishop of York telling me that he was talking to a working man who had given expression to some rather materialist sentiments; and he turned on the young man and challenged him to prove his own existence. To which his only reply was, "Ow, don't talk like that; you make me feel quite funny." Well, of course, some people don't like feeling funny, and try to forget their own existence in the steady contemplation of outward fact. But it won't do; if you have persuaded the dentist to give you a whiff of gas, all that business with the drill can't get itself across; your mind is free-wheeling away in delightful avenues of experience, discovering profound philosophical secrets which it tries to explain to the dentist on waking up, only to find that the secret is just a meaningless string of words. Strictly speaking, if you come to think of it, existence as you know it is divided exactly in half; one half is the things you know and the other half is your mind knowing them.

That we can't fail to realize, the moment we stop to think about it. But what does give us an uncomfortable feeling about this relation of mind to matter is the fact that our minds are so closely wedded to our brains, and through them to our patently material bodies. An accident to the brain can send a man mad for the rest of his life; and there are all sorts of other ways, you can easily think of dozens of them, in which matter seems to have the whip hand over mind; indigestion, drunkenness, drugs, and so on, all affecting the life of the mind through the life of the body. So that it looks as if the mind had to play second fiddle after all; and people who like to use sham-scientific language will not be slow to tell you that the processes of the mind are only a function of the brain. That word "function" is a glorious piece of mumbo-jumbo; it means, in that connection, exactly nothing whatever. It may be true that each mental experience you have is connected with, nay, so far as our present experience goes, is inseparably connected with, some little groove inside one's brain; I wish I could ever learn how to talk scientific language properly. But that isn't to say that your thought is THE SAME THING as the groove in your brain, which would obviously be nonsense. And to say that the one is a function of the other is simply introducing a mathematical term to cover up the nonsense. What does happen, if you come to think of it, when a person goes mad; what do we really know about it? All we know is, that the mind can only receive its impressions, can only express itself, through a mysterious *liaison* with the material body which belongs to it. When that *liaison* is disturbed, I suppose you have the same kind of situation that you have when a deaf organist is playing on an organ in which all the stops are out of tune. He may be the best organist in the world, but the noise that comes out will be simply beastly, because the organ with which he is expressing himself is quite inadequate to his powers of performance. We simply don't know what has happened to the mind; all we know is that there has been an interruption in its sources of communication with the outside world.

But there is another temptation, I think, that most of us have had at times, which makes us think of mind as somehow inferior to matter. I mean the idea that mind is something unnecessary, a sort of additional detail which has somehow blossomed out from matter like flowers from the branches of a tree. Matter is the solid, self-subsistent thing; is mind anything better than a mysterious excrescence on it? And if it's no better than that, shan't we be obliged to admit that matter has a sort of priority over mind? For instance, if all minds suddenly ceased to exist in the world, the world would go on quite happily, with white ants or octopuses or something occupying the position of nature's darling instead of man. Or even if you cut out all sentient life, there would be an interesting struggle to see which weeds overran which. But if you imagine all *matter* suddenly ceasing to exist at this minute, what picture can we form, apart from our theological prepossessions, about what the world would be like? I shouldn't be able to finish off this conference; I should be in a worse position than a deaf man talking to dumb men; I shouldn't even be able to make faces at you. And, of course, there would be even more serious consequences than that. A world of blanks, moving about in a blank world—that is the only picture we can form to ourselves with our present perhaps limited powers of imagination. Mind seems to depend on matter so much; matter to depend on mind so little.

Well, if you think a little deeper, you will see that that argument really tells in exactly the opposite direction. In so far as matter is important to the existence of mind, whereas mind is not important to the existence of matter, in that proportion we are emboldened to say that mind must, in the ultimate constitution of things, have a higher value and importance than matter has. For you can conceive of matter as existing for the sake of mind, whereas you cannot possibly think of mind as existing for the sake of matter. Take those twirligigs in our brains, which are the concomitants, the material coefficient, of our thought. It is possible to suppose that in some way those twirligigs are meant to pave the way for our thoughts, to facilitate our thoughts. Whereas it would be plain nonsense to suppose that our thoughts facilitate, or pave the way for, those twirligigs. The waggling of my tongue, and the twitching of your ears, do subserve an end, though it may not be a very important end, by making it possible for me to transfer my thoughts to your intelligence. But it would be ridiculous to imagine that my thoughts exist for the purpose of making my tongue waggle, or your ears twitch. That which exists for the sake of something else must have less value, in the ultimate nature of things, than that for the sake of which it exists. Pills exist for the sake of health, not health for the sake of pills; which means that health is a more important thing than pills, and so on. And therefore, just in proportion as mind is useless to matter, in that proportion it claims to be a more worth-while thing than matter. So the materialist's boomerang has come back and hit him in the face.

And there is, of course, another very simple and obvious consideration which asserts the priority of mind over matter; I mean the fact that whereas matter can only be the object of thought, mind can be its object as well as its subject. The mind of man, unlike brute matter, unlike even (unless we are strangely deceived in them) the consciousness of other sentient creatures, can turn back upon itself and become self-conscious, become aware of itself as thinking. That which can thus fulfil a double rôle in the scheme of existence must surely have a greater fullness of life and of meaning than that which is confined to a single rôle.

All that, perhaps, may help to allay a scruple which we are apt to get when we hear the scholastic proofs of the existence of God set out. It occurs to us, I mean, to wonder whether the God whose existence philosophy proves is not a kind of abstraction, instead of being a living Person. The proof from order, to be sure, does introduce us to the thought of a Mind by which this order was planned. But when we are told of a Necessary Being, presupposed by all the contingent beings around us, or of a Best which is implied by our better, we are tempted to think of that reality as if it were neuter, as if we ought to talk about IT, not about HIM. But if mind has this priority over matter in the order of being, then there is no question that the ultimate reality must belong to this superior category of Mind, must be, like ourselves, although not with the limitations which the word implies in ourselves, a Person.

There, perhaps, you will expect my meditation to come to an end; you will suppose that I have exhausted all I am capable of saying about mind and matter. But if so, you've forgotten something. Anybody who is in the habit of trying to do cross-words will be familiar with the irritating experience of puzzling for half an hour or so over a clue that just says "ORDER," or "OBJECT," thinking it is a noun, and then suddenly realizing that all the time it was meant to be a verb. In the same way, I told you I was going to give you a meditation on "mind" and "matter"; and I shouldn't have fulfilled my commission if I didn't point out to you that *mind* and *matter* aren't necessarily nouns; they can also be verbs. It's a curious thing, you know, because the English language is not generally supposed to be a good one for expressing philosophical thoughts. And yet as far as I know English is the only language which turns *mind* into a verb and *matter* into a verb. And more than that, although both usages are little better than slang, I think they have a delicate exactness of meaning. Mattering is really connected with what we mean by matter, and minding is really connected with what we mean by mind.

You won't need any profound analysis of what the two verbs do mean. If you are accepting an invitation to dinner, but are anxious to go on to a meeting or a concert or something at nine, you end up your note, "I hope it won't matter if I go just before nine," or "I hope you won't mind if I go just before nine." The sense is, in either case, I hope there is no objection to my going before nine. But we have these two colloquial ways of expressing the same idea, and

we give a slightly different twist to the sentiment according
as we choose one or the other. When we say, "I hope it won't
matter," we hope that it will not transgress against the code of
politeness in general. When we say, "I hope you won't
mind," we hope it is not the kind of action which will tread
on the corns of that particular person. It is only things, you
see, which matter; it is only persons who mind.

Now, in the exchanges of everyday life, I think it will
always be found that when we say, "It doesn't matter," we
always mean, "*I* shan't mind," or "Somebody or other
won't mind." The latter formula is a more exact definition of
our thought. If you say, "It doesn't matter whether I get
through Pass Mods at the end of this term," you mean either
"I don't mind," or "The dons won't mind," or "My people
won't mind." If you say, "It doesn't matter whether I go to
Gloucester via Swindon or via Kingham," you mean either
that the journey takes as long in either case, so you don't
mind, or that your ticket is available for either route, and the
shareholders of the G.W.R., who are enriched in either case,
don't mind. Mattering, in the ordinary affairs of life, is always
related to somebody's convenience; it is always, in the long
run, a person you are thinking of, a person who minds.

But you can use the verb "to matter" in what would
appear to be an absolute, not a relative sense. For instance,
somebody may ask you, "Do you think it really matters, if I
get drunk?" Well, of course, he may simply mean, "Will
the dean mind, if he finds me breaking lamps?" Or he may
simply mean, "Would you say from your experience that *I*
shall mind much if I have a hangover next morning?" But
the presumption on which you answer his question is a
perfectly different one. You presume him to mean, "Is there
some permanent moral law which will be violated, some equi-
librium in the nature of things (not merely in my own mind)
which will be disturbed, if I get drunk?" For once, it seems,

we have got away from the personal reference; there are things which really matter in themselves, independently of whether somebody minds or not. If we say that it matters a great deal when Hitler starts persecuting the Jews, we don't simply mean that the Jews mind; of course they mind. And we don't simply mean that the *News Chronicle* minds, because the *News Chronicle* is not our ultimate test of human values. We mean that there is some order of justice external to himself which Hitler is violating. The thing matters IN ITSELF.

But, when you come to think of it, can a thing matter in itself? That is where you come up against a fresh argument for the existence of God; the argument from conscience. I call it a fresh argument, because it is not explicitly stated among the five scholastic proofs; though, of course, you can say, if you like, that it is only a particular development of the argument from degrees of being. If you put it in its crude form, the argument from conscience runs, I suppose, like this: "I find, in my conscience, a law telling me to do this and that, forbidding me to do this and that; there is no law without a law-giver; hence a supreme Law-giver must exist, whom we call God." But the form in which I should prefer to put it, for the purposes of this meditation, is the question, "Can anything matter, unless there is Somebody who minds?"

You see, the difficulty is not really confined to the moral order. How can there be any absolute Truth, unless it be the Truth which is in God? How can there be any such thing as beauty, with a power of its own to compel our homage, unless it be a reflection of the Beauty which is in God? But it is in the moral order that we recognize the difficulty most, because the moral order affects every decision of our wills. How can I rest content with saying that loving my neighbour, or following the path of duty, or respecting my own body, is something which MATTERS, if that is all the account that can be given of it? It would mean that I, a person, am being ordered about and tyrannized over by a thing—my conscience. And that thing, my conscience, is a part of myself. Or, if you prefer to talk about duty instead of conscience, you are worse off still; I, a concrete person, am being ordered about by a thing which is an abstraction. Don't let us fall into the error of saying that I don't obey my conscience, but the general conscience of humanity. That is what these modern people are always trying to do; I got a letter only the other day from somebody who wanted me to sign a letter protesting against the persecution of the Jews "before the conscience of civilization." But civilization is an abstraction, and it hasn't got a conscience. What they mean is, a collection of consciences belonging to a collection of civilized people; just as when they talk about the universal mind they only mean a collection of individual minds. But I don't want to appeal to my own conscience or to anybody else's conscience; I want to appeal to Somebody who minds, and has a right to mind, whenever the moral law is infringed; and he who minds must be a Person. Short of that, I cannot make sense of the proposition that anything matters. I cannot see how any mere *thing* has the right to abridge the liberties of myself, who am a person.

That is the argument from conscience as I see it; not, I'm afraid, put to you with due forms of philosophical discussion. Of course, in the very last analysis, the thing is not as simple as all that. I mean, it would be easy for somebody to pose me with the difficulty: "Do you mean sin only matters because God happens to mind? That murder, for example, is not something wrong in itself, and God, if he had preferred it that way, might just as well have commanded, Thou *shalt* commit murder, as the other way round?" To that I suppose I should reply, that in the last mysterious analysis "it matters" and "he minds" are, in God, the same thing. Things aren't good just because God wills them, nor does God will things just because they are good. Goodness is his own Nature, that is, himself. But if there were no *he*, if there were only an *it*, to dictate commands to free moral beings like ourselves, could we reconcile ourselves to the indignity of it? I know I couldn't.

III

IF GOD EXISTS——

LET me suggest this point to you—that God, not man, must be the measure of the Universe, must be the standard by which we are to judge all our experience. If we make man the centre of all our experience, then the riddle of existence becomes insoluble, and we had far better give it up.

Aristotle said that Man is the measure of all things. You see, you must have a fixed point somewhere for the start of every investigation, a unit somewhere for the standard of every computation. I seem to remember that when they taught me science, they made me learn by heart a long formula, which said, "A gramme is the weight of a cubic centimetre of pure water, kept at a temperature of something or other Centigrade, at the latitude of Paris, on the level of the sea, *in vacuo*." Now, that seems to me very sensible, although it might be more useful to me if I could remember what the temperature was. If you are going to weigh everything in the world by grammes, you must have a fixed standard of what the gramme is; otherwise you will find that on one occasion you have used your cubic centimetre of pure water when it was frozen, and at another time when it was liquid, and at another time when it was half evaporated, and all your calculations will be miles out in consequence. In fact you will be very much in the position of the people in *Alice in*

Wonderland, trying to play croquet with flamingoes for mallets and hedgehogs for croquet-balls; the flamingoes were always curling their necks round and the hedgehogs were always running away, so that you never got much further. You must have a mallet which moves only when you make it move; you must have a croquet-ball which stays put until you hit it, or the game is not croquet. In the same way, all measurement and all thought depend on the possession of a fixed unit by which your judgments can be compared.

Now, if you deny the existence of God, or if you deny it for practical purposes by treating it as a fifty-fifty probability, or if you use the word "God" in an insincere way, meaning a mere abstraction or a mere ideal when you use it, then you have to say that man is the measure of all things; that his thought is the highest form of wisdom which exists, that his conscience is the standard by which good and evil must be determined, that his intuitions are the only test of beauty. And indeed more than that; if you are to attain any kind of intellectual satisfaction, you must say that man's thought is the source of all truth, *makes* things true; that his conscience is the arbiter of good, *makes* things right and wrong; that his intuitions are the origin of all beauty, *make* things beautiful or ugly. And that notion, if you press it, leads to mere intellectual despair.

Man's thought is not a fixed thing. It is not merely that men disagree with one another; one generation of men sees things in a different light from the generations which went before it. There are fashions in human thought; mechanism was the keyword of the century before last, evolution of the century that has just gone, relativity of our own. Philosophy goes round in circles, now realism will be the dominant teaching, now idealism, now pragmatism; there is no fixed point, we are always changing. And always when the recognition or God's existence becomes obscured in the public consciousness, thought turns back upon itself, and wonders whether it has any validity, and we are worse off than ever. After all, if a person refuses to believe in the existence of a world outside himself, and thinks that all his experience is a mere illusion, it is impossible to prove to him that he is wrong. If he says that two and two make five, or that time and space are a hallucination, it is impossible to prove to him that he is wrong. The human mind is as tortuous as any flamingo, as volatile as any hedgehog. And we are asked, not merely to believe that this uncertain instrument is all we have to judge our experience by—which is in a sense true—but that it is actually this erratic, eccentric mind of ours which *gives* things their truth, which *makes* things true. Whereas if you believe in God you know that God is Truth, and gives to all things that exist the truth that is in them, and gives to all minds, according to their measure, some knowledge, although it be an imperfect knowledge, of the truth which he sees in the mirror of his own eternal being, perfectly as it is.

Man's conscience is not a fixed thing either. If you took a referendum of England now, you would probably find that in the majority of English minds war is something in itself wicked*; if you had taken it twelve years ago you would have found only a fanatical minority supporting that contention. A hundred years ago, people thought of divorce as something disgraceful; now, most people do not think of it as disgraceful at all. Some people want us to think that the only criterion of right and wrong action is the comfort or discomfort of our fellow-men, of the community at large; others, that we decide between right and wrong by a kind of artistic intuition; others, that conscience is a voice we must obey implicitly without asking why. Now, you will have a precious hard time making up your mind between right and wrong nowadays if you even treat your own unaided

* This was, I think, true at the time I wrote it.

conscience as the judge of them. But we are asked to believe more than that; we are asked to believe that this uncertain instrument, the human conscience, is not merely the oracle which tells you whether a thing is right or wrong, but actually the authority which makes some things right and others wrong. Whereas if you believe in God you know that God is goodness, that he imparts to all things which exist the good that is in them; that he gives to our hearts, though in a differing and an inferior measure, some appreciation of that Goodness which he sees perfectly mirrored and summed up in himself.

And so, still more obviously, with our intuitions about other things, our artistic judgments for example. That men's tastes in beauty differ is a thing which has in every age been notorious; if you doubt it, you have only to go and look at the Underground Station in Piccadilly. Is there such a thing as absolute beauty? If so, the human mind has taken a precious long time in deciding what it is like. And yet if there is no such thing as absolute beauty, the whole of art and music become a matter of mere individual caprice. And then the psychologists come in on the top of that, and explain that all our judgments of beauty are really due to processes in our unconscious minds, and rather unprintable processes at that. If you rule out God, these faulty, inconsistent intuitions of ours are not merely the only standard by which beauty can be judged; it is they that create beauty, that make things beautiful—what nonsense it all is! Whereas if you believe in God, you believe that he himself is absolute beauty, and gives beauty to all things in this creation, and to our eyes and senses the power to see and to appreciate it.

Now, all these considerations I have been suggesting to you are not reasons why we should believe that God exists, but rather reasons for wanting him to exist. At least, there are people who would try to prove the existence of God in this way, but I should not like to depend merely on such proofs myself. They are rather reasons for *wanting* God to exist. "If there were no God, it would be necessary to invent one," as Voltaire said, if it was Voltaire who said that. The reasons for asserting the existence of God are reasons derived from the very nature of the world as we know it. If the created Universe were a mere lump of inert matter, lying about in space with no visible means of subsistence, we might perhaps feel inclined to give up the problem of how it got there although even its presence seems to demand the intervention of a Creator, of somebody or something which exists in its own right, instead of merely happening to be there. But when, from this lump of matter, a vegetable life emerges which was not there before, and from that vegetable life animal life, and from that animal life conscious life, the life of the mind, all with no natural reason to account for it beyond a mere chance juxtaposition of atoms—then our reason does demand that there should be an agent at work, producing the things that were not from the things that are. It is no good saying that life was potentially present from the first; we still need some agent to bring that potency into act; life did not evolve itself, because until it had evolved it was not yet alive. Or alternatively, we discover, we are still discovering in the world of our experience, laws, infinitely subtle and delicate in their operation, which govern the ways of nature. Our minds, with great difficulty, can discover those laws, but they did not make those laws, they did not put them there—they find them there. And since law and order can only be the expression of a mind, we have to believe in the existence of a Mind which invented those laws and imposed them upon brute nature. And so once more we find it necessary to believe in a Creative Intelligence, that is in God.

But now, you see, in proving the existence of God we find that we have gone further, and proved a whole lot of things

2

about God. All the attributes of God, his simplicity, his immutability and so on, are not something which we learn from the Bible, or from the tradition of the Church, they are something which we learn from reason itself, learn from that same process of reasoning by which we prove that God exists. It is no good asserting the existence of a Creator who is not omnipotent; for if he is not omnipotent he is limited—who or what is it that limits him? You will have to fall back on assuming the existence of some power greater than that of the Creator himself. It is no good asserting the existence of a God who is not simple, who is in any way composite; for if so you will have to fall back on assuming the existence of some power which produced that fusion of elements in him. And so on all through; the proofs from which we learn the existence of God give us some idea, necessarily, of his Nature.

Many muddle-headed people who think they cannot get on without God, if they really sat down to argue out the question of his existence, would find that they had let themselves in for a good deal more than they bargained for. They want God to exist as a sort of background to their lives; they want to feel that there is a supreme truth in which all our imperfect guesses after truth find their meaning; that there is a supreme Goodness towards which all our feeble moral effort strives; that there is a beauty which is beyond all earthly beauty, and is the explanation of it. That is what they mean by God; that is what they are wanting when they say they want God. But if they would only try to puzzle out the mystery of his Being they would find that he is a great deal more than that. They would find that he is a Personal Being, infinitely removed in dignity from this universe, his created handiwork; outside all time and all space; not limited, as we are limited, by imperfections of nature; not composite as we are composite, not changeable as we are changeable; the Creator of all things, and such a Creator as not only gave them being but maintains them, from moment to moment, in being; who made them all for his glory, yet would have lacked nothing of that eternal blessedness which he enjoys if nothing had ever existed outside himself. That is the God they would find, if they would look for him; for whom they will not look because they are afraid of finding him.

They wanted God to exist as a sort of background to their lives; but if you once prove that he exists, you will find that he fills the whole stage. Man is no longer the centre of the Universe—God is the centre of the Universe. Man is no longer the measure of all things, God is the measure of all things. All the greatness of man, all his splendid achievements in art and in music and in learning and in the conquest of nature, in laws and governments, in heroism and endurance, fade away into the background and become something very insignificant, when they are seen in contrast with the incommunicable Majesty of Almighty God. Lord, what is man, that thou rememberest him, or the son of man, that thou visitest him? So brief his existence, so puny his stature, so limited the possibilities of his being.

And it is not merely that God, once we have caught some hint of what he is, fills the whole picture and dwarfs his own creatures by the contrast. We begin to see, too, that God has claims upon man, which know of no limits and admit of no qualifications. We are God's creatures, drawn by him out of nothing, and ready, but for the continued exercise of his power, to fall back into that nothingness whence we came; his dominion over us is absolute, and all his kindness in his dealings with us springs from the goodness of his own nature, not from any rights, not from any value, of ours. And having such dominion over us, he will expect from us love and worship and service, unquestioning obedience to his will for us; he will want to be the end of all our actions, as he is the end of all created things. So that our actions will no longer be regulated by our own measure, but by his. We shall not need to ask, "Is this course of action profitable to me, is it pleasant to me, is it worthy of me, is it a true expression of my own nature, is it the kind of action I myself should approve in my calmer moments, will it leave my character the nobler for its effects?" No, all those calculations, based upon human pride, will be superseded, will be put on one side; there is only one question which will be the ultimate rule of conduct—"Is this course of action the course of action by which it is God's will to be glorified in me?"

For us Catholics, and for all those who take their religion seriously, this sense of the overwhelming Majesty of God is the first consideration, comes before, even, our sense of his love and of his mercy; our God is a jealous God, is a consuming Fire; there is nothing we can do for him that we do not owe to him, no praise of him which can seem extravagant, no self-abasement before him which can seem undignified. In saying that God exists, we have admitted that he is everything, that man is nothing. To realize that unique Majesty of his, to realize this pitiable nothingness of ours—that is the disposition into which, if we have followed them, this term's conferences ought to lead us.

IV

WHITE-WASHING CALIBAN

E have been discussing the possibility of proving the existence of God by the use of our natural reason. There are arguments, and cogent arguments, by which that doctrine can be demonstrated without any recourse to a revelation, either to such an imperfect revelation as was given to the Jews through Moses, or to the perfect revelation which has been given to us in these later times through our Lord Jesus Christ. But there is a fresh difficulty which confronts us now, even if it has not occurred to some of us already. Granted that it is possible for *us* to make such inferences from what we know about ourselves and about the nature of the world around us, was it equally possible for man to do so long centuries ago, when he was far less developed intellectually, when all his mental energies were devoted to getting food and dodging the wild beasts, and he had no time for speculative thinking? Even as things are, I felt that some of you were looking a little blank when you were being confronted with the argument from contingent being. And yet there is nobody in this congregation who does not possess at least a rudimentary aptitude for discursive thought. What would the hairy Ainu make of it, or the South African bushman, if we started talking to him about essence and existence? He would be a non-starter, surely, from the first.

And yet, if primitive man was not in a position to form

some kind of ideas about God, and man's relation to God, and man's duties in the sight of God, how are we to reconcile that with the notion that all men are responsible to God for their actions, and will be judged by him according to the efforts they made to live according to his will? Had they really any chance—the people who died before any Christian missionaries could get at them? And if not, how do we reconcile that with the goodness or even with the justice of God? Such questions agitated Catholic thinkers a good deal about a hundred years ago; naturally. Because it was about a hundred years ago that people began to wake up to the fact that human life on this planet went back a long way beyond the four thousand years or so that Archbishop Ussher had allowed to it. It was in 1825 that Kent's Cavern, near Torquay, was first scientifically examined, and the theory brought forward that the remains there proved the coexistence of man with animals which were extinct before history began. As you probably know, by an odd chance it was the local Catholic priest, a certain Father McEnery, who gave this theory to the world, and was immediately told that that was all nonsense; it didn't in the least agree with the best theories of the best people. However, palæontology got going, and it became generally realized that for thousands of years before Moses there were human beings going about the world who must, theologically speaking, have had immortal souls. And two ways were devised of explaining how these people might have had a chance of knowing, and therefore of loving and worshipping God. One, which is properly described as Fideism, is to suppose that every human soul has, if it will but enter into itself, an intuitive knowledge of God's existence, just as every soul has an intuitive power of distinguishing between right and wrong; that a kind of interior revelation is thus offered to every soul, however deeply sunk in ignorance or heathenism. The other, properly called Traditionalism, supposes that there has been, at all times, a tradition handed down from Adam to his posterity; instead of an individual revelation to each human soul, you would thus have a common revelation made once for all to the human race, which, although it has become obscured at various times, and in various places, has never been allowed to die out.

Both those doctrines were condemned by the Council of the Vatican, not on their positive but on their negative side. There is no reason why you should not believe, if you want to believe, that every man born into the world is privileged with a direct intuition of God's existence, although it does not seem to be borne out much by our common experience. Nor is there any reason why a continuous tradition on the subject should not have existed from the time of the first human pair right down to our own day, in some part of the world; very probably it has, although evidently it has been very much overgrown with false beliefs. No, what the Church insists on is this, that it is theoretically possible for any human being, even at a low stage of development, to find out God for himself if he will use the natural gift of reason which God has given him. Actually, in innumerable cases the traditions in which he has been brought up, or the psychological influences which have affected him, will make it almost impossible that he should; and we cannot but believe that God will judge, in such cases, with a mercy proportionate to the lack of opportunity. But you mustn't say that the knowledge of God's existence can *only* come to us through a revelation, public or private; that there is no other way in which such an idea could ever have been entertained; that is heresy.

Meanwhile, I need hardly say that the question, "How does man come to entertain the idea of God?" has been discussed for the last hundred years by people outside the Church from a very different point of view. These people assume that God does not exist, and having made that assumption they proceed to consider how such an illusion can have arisen, on Aristotle's principle that you should not be content with proving your adversary to be in error; you should find out the explanation of how the error arose. And indeed most of the agnostic writers you come across nowadays are so busy providing explanations of how men came to believe in God, that they omit altogether to consider whether his existence is or is not a fact. Anthropologists have held various theories about the origin of religion during this last century, and I haven't time to distinguish them, but roughly you can say that the theory which has most recently enjoyed popularity is this. In the first instance, they say, primitive man has a sense of something holy or something mysterious attaching to certain things; he believes in a kind of impersonal power which is connected with particular spots or particular objects or particular occupations. Then he begins to personify these spiritual influences and give them names; he comes to believe in the existence of separate spirits, living spirits like himself, dwelling in or behind certain objects—his family hearth, for example, or his fruit trees, or his cattle sheds. And then among these multitudinous deities of his one comes to the front, achieves special importance; perhaps first of all it is the earth-mother, then it will be the sun-god, and last of all it will be the sky-god, a being who lives right up above the clouds. And when primitive man has got to that point he is in a position to drop his belief in the other gods, as the Jews did when they came out of Egypt, and become a monotheist. It's much more complicated than that, but those are the broad outlines of anthropological doctrine as it was till lately and as it is still in the handbooks. And if you get into discussion with anybody who has been reading anthropology he will feed that sort of stuff to you.

When you asked these people how they knew that that was the way in which theology developed, or how they knew that it had developed at all, you found the situation was rather curious. They assumed that there had been a development, because they were under the spell of evolutionary doctrine. Some forms of culture, some religious ideas, some ceremonies, appeared to them to be more complicated and therefore more highly developed than others; therefore, they said, these were later than the others, and the savage tribes among whom they were found must be considered a later form of civilization than those savage tribes in which they did not appear. So, you see, they were cooking their facts all the time. They would tell you that the sky-god only appeared in late civilizations like the Yahoo, or whatever it might be; and when you looked back to an earlier page to find out why the Yahoos were thought to be a late civilization, you found it was because they believed in the sky-god. The whole thing was theory, with no relation to ascertainable fact at all. One man protested against this, a fellow-countryman of our own, and one of the most interesting; Andrew Lang. He kept on pointing out the strong probability that they had got it all the wrong way round; that belief in a personal deity came first, and that the other religious business, the myths and the magic and the totems and all the rest of it, were developments or degenerations which grew up later. And they all said, "Ah, that paradoxical fellow Lang! What joke will he be springing on us next?"

Then, just recently, Lang's protest has been taken up by a very different kind of person; Dr Schmidt, a priest who used to hold the chair of ethnology, I think it is, in Vienna university. He was up here some years ago, giving some lectures at Manchester, for he is a man of world-wide reputation, and has been president of the ethnological congress and editor of *Anthropos*, which is the trade organ of the anthropologists, and I don't know what besides. And he started out on a quite original plan. He would determine from other considerations, from race, from geographical distribution, from the nature of the implements they used and from their general standard of culture, which of the savage tribes known to us were really the earliest, the very very earliest. And then, having satisfied himself about this, he would see whether these really primitive tribes had or had not got the kind of religious attitude which Tylor and Fraser and all the rest of them described as "primitive."

I am simply boiling down for you this morning the substance of his book *The Origin and Growth of Religion*. He draws up a list of the people, scattered about in odd corners of the globe, who can be described as really primitive. One very obvious test he applies, which narrows the range of candidates considerably; Which are the Food-gatherers? The people, that is, who have never, or never till demonstrably recent times, cultivated the earth or raised cattle at all; who have lived simply on what they could get by hunting and on the fruits they could pick wild? And there are other tests, of course—the use of the bow, any at all developed use of pottery, any power of working metals, everything like that disqualifies a people from being thought of as really primitive.

He finds these primitive peoples, as I say, in odd pockets up and down the world. He finds them in the south-east of Australia, in Tierra del Fuego at the very south of the American Continent, among the pygmies in Africa, in the Andaman Islands, among the Eskimos, in some Californian tribes of North America, and so on. Of course, in many cases you find that these people have taken over in part the ideas and the habits of their slightly more civilized neighbours. But so far as you can isolate their real native character, these tribes and a few more give you a fairly consistent picture of what mankind must have been like before the fields were ever tilled, or cattle were ever tamed, when only the rudest of tools and of implements had even been invented.

Observe that the very isolation of these peoples proves the genuineness of their traditions. If, 2,000 years hence, some ethnologist investigated the remains of England and proved that whereas the vast bulk of its savage population wore loin-cloths, but just in a few parts, in Cornwall and in the Lakes and on the coast of Norfolk, men were found wearing trousers, he would be perfectly justified in saying that the common tradition of these few isolated districts, which had no communication with each other, was unmistakable evidence. It would mean that originally British people wore trousers, and that loin-cloths, as worn in all the central part of the island, were the innovation. So with these pygmies and bushmen. Whatever culture they possess in common they have not learned from one another; how could they, scattered as they are? Therefore it is something that has come down to them from days, long centuries ago, when they and people like them populated the whole world. There's another interesting point. Assuming—and it seems all the evidence we have justifies us in assuming—that human life began in and spread from Central Asia, you will see that these primitive peoples have been driven, by the continuous pressure of other civilizations more powerful than themselves, into the remotest corners of the world; just as the Celts of our own island have been driven into the remotest corners of our own island—the highlands of Scotland, Wales, Cornwall. So you find these people in the south of Australia, in the south of Africa, in the south of America, in remote islands of the Indian Ocean that lead nowhere, on the fringe of the Arctic Circle, in the narrow strip of land that stretches along northern America, shut off between the mountains and the sea. You find the really primitive peoples where you would expect to find them, in the corners into which their conquerors pushed them while the going was good.

Now, let me summarize quite briefly the findings of Dr

Schmidt about the religious ideas of these primitive peoples, supported by a whole mass of evidence in a much longer book which he is slowly bringing out. Not each point, of course, is true about each tribe, but this is the general picture. All the things we think of as very queer and primitive, totems, and cannibalism, and earth-goddesses, and magic, and solar myths, and the vegetation-spirit, and human sacrifice, and all the things the anthropologists have been making such play with this century past, are not really primitive at all. They are later innovations, belonging to the ages when men tilled the ground and shot beasts with arrows and grazed cattle and did civilized things like that. Among the really primitive peoples all the odd, fantastic elements of savage religion either don't occur at all, or only occur here and there, in a half-hearted way. Meanwhile, all these early peoples believe in one God. Sometimes they have a collection of other deities, but always there is one top god, so to speak, quite unmistakably superior to anything else that exists in their thought. He lives in the sky; he is the creator of everything in the world, and generally of the sky itself as well. Sometimes the existence of evil in the world is attributed to a second being, the Coyote, for example, of the American Indians; but he is a sort of corner-man, like Brer Fox in Uncle Remus, and he is always utterly inferior to the Creator. The Creator is all good, and approves of, indeed exacts, right behaviour among men. I may add that among these primitives monogamy is very definitely the rule. They pray to the Creator, though some of them more than others; there is an Arctic people with an unpronounce-able name who say they do not pray much, because the white people are always praying and it doesn't seem to them much good. They offer sacrifices from their hunting, but not human sacrifices at all. The Creator is always personal; he is ordinarily represented as Omniscient, Omnipotent, and Eternal. Now, all that is not really a bad morning's

work for people who have never learned to shoot with a
bow or turn the earth with a plough. I daresay they would
not exactly follow an argument about essence and existence;
but they have preserved, from an age long, long before
history began, the cult of a God who, in all essential features,
strongly resembles the God we Christians worship. I should
add that all these peoples without exception believe in
survival after death, and several of them in a world of
rewards and punishments hereafter.

Well, all this working back into the past is an uncertain
business, and lends itself to continual shifting between one
theory and another. I don't pretend that what Dr Schmidt
tells us is in any way final; he doesn't pretend it himself.
But it is clear, I think, that just at the moment* the latest and
the most fruitful anthropological research is all on the side of
the angels. So that if you get into an argument which runs on
these lines, it will be a fairly safe way of closuring the
discussion to say, "I suppose you have read Dr Schmidt?"

* Written in 1932.

V

UNDER PONTIUS PILATE

WE have been talking about natural theology; that is, about the knowledge of God which man can reach for himself, if he will trust his own reason and his own conscience. The next stage in apologetic is to establish, on historical grounds, the fact that our Lord came to earth and that he claimed to bring a fuller revelation from God; the grounds, too, on which he justified that claim.

First of all let's get this point clear—that God wasn't *bound* to reveal himself to man. In spite of our dual nature, in spite of the Fall, man has got enough apparatus left to serve God, if he wants to, without any direct supernatural assistance. His reason will tell him that God exists, if he will only think. His conscience will tell him that God ought to be obeyed, and, in general outline, what are the laws which God wants him to obey, if he will only listen to it. We believe, in fact, that it is possible for a man brought up altogether remote from Christian influence and therefore, through no fault of his own, a heathen or practically a heathen, to reach heaven if he will make use of the actual graces God sends him, by being sorry for his sins and so on. And we should have no grievance against God, in strict justice at least, if all of us were in the same position; if you and I had never been brought up in the Catholic faith, if (for that matter) there had been no Catholic faith for us to be brought up in.

That's all perfectly true, but it doesn't need a very profound study of human nature to discover that most men, left to the light of their natural reason and conscience, don't, at least to all appearance, put up much of a show. The human reason is curiously apt to get warped in such a way that it only thinks what it wants to think; the human conscience is even more prone to accommodate itself, so that a man comes to approve of himself for doing exactly the thing he wants to do. We make exceptions; we tell ourselves that circumstances alter cases. Like the South Sea Islander, you remember, in Mark Twain, who was very much impressed when he was told the story of Cain and Abel, but when the missionary tried to improve the occasion by going on to say that Cain was a South Sea Islander, he rather altered his point of view, and said, "What was Abel fooling around there for, anyway?" I always like that phrase in the *Imitation of Christ* which compares our natural reason to a spark left among the ashes— you know, that irritating bit of live coal which makes it *look* as if it ought to be possible to get the fire going again by just drawing it with a newspaper, but when you've tried it for about half an hour you find that you have to ring for the housemaid and get her to lay the fire afresh after all. That, as we know, is what our Lord's Incarnation meant, the *remaking* of our nature. And, so far as our reason is concerned, he did that in the first place by making to us a revelation of the Divine Nature; by telling us and showing us more about God than we knew, more than we ever could have known, by any philosophical speculation.

More than we ever could have known—whereas reason merely teaches us that God is One, revelation informs us there are three Persons in one Godhead; whereas the doctrine of Purgatory was something the human reason might have guessed at (and indeed, some of the pagans, notably Virgil, made an uncommonly good shot at it) only revelation could have established its truth, and so on. To bring us such information, we need a Messenger from God; an Ambassador, and one who can present credentials to us, so that we can be sure he comes from God. Remember, it is not logically necessary for us, at this stage in apologetics, to prove that Jesus Christ was the Son of God; all we want to be sure of at this stage is that he is God's Ambassador to man. Revelation might have come to us through an angel; might have come to us, even, through the granting of special illumination to an ordinary human being. That God's Ambassador should be God himself is an extra, something we could not have claimed or covenanted for. But the Ambassador must have credentials; we must be able to distinguish the revelation which he brings from all the bogus revelations which are splashed across the pages of history; Mahomet with his book, Joanna Southcott with her sealed box, Joseph Smith with his gold plates, and so on. Nay, we must be able to distinguish it from merely private revelations, such as those given to St Theresa and St Margaret Mary, which, though we believe them to be divine in their origin, were nevertheless *private* revelations, not imposing belief on anybody except the persons themselves to whom they were made. There must be evidence for all to see.

That—I think you can say it without irreverence—is the minimum we could be satisfied with, if we were to have a revelation at all. But there are plenty of people—you will probably have come across them among those fellow-students of yours with whom you conduct theological arguments at about two o'clock in the morning—who say they want *more* than that. They say, for example, if God really meant to reveal himself, in this solemn and convincing way, to mankind, why should that revelation come to mankind at a particular point in the history of our race? Why should God's Ambassador only appear on earth for a matter of thirty years, exercise his preaching ministry only over the space of a short three years, and that such a very long time ago? Or alternatively, if it was to happen at one particular point in time, why couldn't it have happened in our own day, or somewhere rather nearer our own day, so that it could have been verified by more trained observation, and enshrined in more accurate records?

Well, the immediate answer to that is quite a simple one—that since, as we have seen, revelation is not something to which we could have laid claim as a right, *a fortiori* we have no right to say we want a revelation of this or that kind, in excess of the bare logical minimum. To be sure, a revelation which was incapable of producing conviction would be almost worse than nothing; it would be a continual worry to us without in any way enabling us to make up our minds. But to say that we will not look at any revelation which does not come to us with headlines, so to speak, all across the page, shouting its message at us, compelling attention and forcing conviction on us—that would be presumptuous, seeing what we are. Beggars, after all, cannot be choosers.

And although we have very limited opportunities of understanding the principles on which God acts in his dealings with us, this at least seems certain from all we know of his operations, that he doesn't work miracles unnecessarily. He practises a kind of economy, raising up a saint only here and there, granting a great deliverance only now and again, working according to the laws which govern his natural creation for the most part, and only superseding them within narrow limits. He might, I suppose, have arranged that every Pope should start performing miracles immediately upon his election, and marked out the Holy See in that way as the infallible oracle for the solution of all our difficulties. But, as far as we can see, that is not God's way; that's all there is to be said about it. He won't make things TOO easy for us, in this world of our probation; won't lavish his supernatural favours in a degree which might make them become cheap and stale to us. He preferred to concentrate our attention on a particular historical figure; a Man as we ourselves are men. He preferred to let the supernatural world break through into ours at a particular period in time, as we men are bounded and conditioned by periods of time. We were to live by faith; deriving from the very obscurity in which faith works the opportunity for showing our loyalty to him, believing where we have not seen.

Meanwhile, we must think twice before we quarrel with the particular period of time which he chose for that Divine event. It's perfectly true, of course, that in our day we have much more apparatus for recording events than the human race had nineteen hundred years ago. If some doubt should arise, years hence, about the exact circumstances of King George's funeral, it would be possible, I suppose, to turn up all sorts of films and gramophone records, and the files of innumerable papers, so that all controversy could be set at rest. And in the same way, any alleged miracle at Lourdes can be tested by the doctors there far more accurately than our Lord's miracles were in his day. But then, in the first place, you can't be certain that if the Church hadn't been there to revive the tradition of learning when the barbarians came, the achievements of modern science would have been possible. And further, when you complain in this way that Almighty God was in too much of a hurry to reveal himself, you forget that there are plenty of people who make precisely the opposite complaint, and ask why he did not reveal himself sooner. Why all those thousands of years between the Fall and the Incarnation? Why must Abraham, and Moses, and David, why must Confucius, and Buddha, and Socrates, live and die without having the chance of gaining that enlightenment which our Lord came to bring?

After all, the world at large *had* been prepared, in a very special way, for our Lord's coming. And that applies, not only to the conditions of human thought, but to the ordinary conditions of life as well. The known world, for practical purposes, united under a single Government; a common language, the Greek language, and a common civilization, the Greek civilization, spread in every part of it; an admirable system of roads for transport; great facility in writing, and in the copying of manuscripts; a quite unexampled interval of peace, in the East especially—after all, if our Lord had come seventy years earlier he would have found Jerusalem being captured by Pompey, if he had come seventy years later he would have found it being destroyed by Titus. All those conditions, you will see for yourself, were perfect conditions as far as they went for the diffusion of a new world-idea. Virgil's fourth eclogue shows that the world was ready for it, just when the Jewish people, with the prophecy of Daniel in its hands, was full of expectation that the long-promised deliverance would be accomplished.

But there's another difficulty which is sometimes expressed, and perhaps felt more often than it is expressed; I mean the question why our Lord, granted that he preferred to come at the time when he came, should have come to Palestine, rather than to some more fashionable and influential part of the world. We all know, I hope, that there is a devotional meaning in our Lord's choice of obscure surroundings when he came to earth. But that doesn't concern us this morning; we are dealing with the question as a matter of apologetics. Was Palestine, we ask, the right centre for the diffusion of a world-idea, at a moment when the Roman Empire was at its zenith, and nothing that happened outside Rome could really rivet the attention of mankind?

The answer is that it was. The Jewish people was, and is, unique. The Jews alone in the ancient world had preserved the tradition that there is one true God. Oh, I know they were always falling short of that standard, and relapsing into idolatry; but they always came back to their origins, drove out the false idea, and confessed their shortcomings. And if they were unique in their faith, they were unique also in their hope. Alone among the nations of the world, they looked forward to the future instead of looking back to the past; the expected coming of a Redeemer was an integral part of the philosophy by which they lived. That faith and that hope combined with, and helped to form, an intensely nationalistic feeling among them which made it impossible, and (some would say) still makes it impossible to merge them in the common stock of mankind. Ask yourself what an ancient Roman or an ancient Greek, a Babylonian or an Assyrian looked like, and you will have to go to the sculptures in a museum to find out. Ask yourself what an ancient Jew looked like, and you have only got to go to the jeweller's round the corner. They preserved then, as they preserve now, their obstinate nationality.

And, with these characteristics, then as now, they were scattered over the face of the earth. "There were, dwelling in Jerusalem, Jews, devout men, from every nation under heaven," so the Acts of the Apostles describe the day of Pentecost, and it was true; since the captivity in Babylon, they had spread everywhere. I shouldn't wonder if there were as many Jews, then, in the single city of Alexandria, as there are in Great Britain to-day. And they kept up communications with one another; you can see that all over the Acts, all over St Paul's epistles. Well, I won't say that that made the preaching of the Gospel easier; as we know, in many cases it was the Jews who were, at first, the chief enemies of the new religion. But it made it certain that the Christian claim would be discussed everywhere, that the Christian missionaries would be known everywhere. If our Lord had come to Rome instead of Palestine, to Rome, that Babylon of strange creeds and shifting opinions, humanly speaking his career would have been a nine days' wonder. In coming to Palestine, he struck at the religious nerve-centre of the human race.

In saying all that, I haven't been trying to establish the truth of the Christian revelation. The fact that it came into the world at a moment, and in circumstances, which favoured its rapid diffusion is not, so far, evidence that it was true. No, this morning I've only been attempting to deal with a negative objection—the objection that there is no need to pay any attention to the Christian claim, because the events which tend to substantiate it happened in such a hole-and-corner way, happened such a long time ago. I've been trying to show that *that* criticism at any rate is shallow and ill-founded, if only you will take an unprejudiced view of history.

And there's one thing that's worth adding about the records themselves; I mean, those New Testament documents to which, treated merely as historical documents, our apologetic makes its appeal. They *are* historical records, of unusual value. The manuscripts themselves are very much nearer in date to their originals than most manuscripts which deal with the events of the ancient world. When you are dealing with the secular events of the same period, your chief authority is the Annals of Tacitus. And the oldest MS. we possess of Tacitus' Annals comes down to us from the tenth, or just possibly the ninth century. But the Codex Sinaiticus, about which we all heard so much when it was bought for the nation a few years ago, dates from the fourth century; and we have other MSS. of the same or nearly the same date. I was told the other day that they have now found a MS. of some of St Paul's epistles which goes back a whole century behind Sinaiticus. And, of course, there are the papyrus fragments, still earlier, and the quotations in the fathers, which help us to determine the exact state of the text. And the Gospel records themselves are, or purport to be, sober historical records, not high-flown poetry like the early records of most other religions. The first three Gospels, whatever may be said of the fourth, were certainly written within the lifetime of many people who had witnessed the events they record, and were in a position to contradict their statements if they had a mind to. There is no reason to quarrel with them, merely as records, any more than with the commentaries of Cæsar, or the life of Tiberius which was written by Velleius Paterculus. Whatever inferences you draw from their contents, you cannot, without forfeiting your claim to be regarded as a serious critic, treat them otherwise than as history.

And I say we are going to treat them merely as history. Don't ever allow yourself to be taken in by that stale old piece of slander, that we Catholics first give the authority of the Church as our ground for believing that the Bible is free from error, and then give the inerrancy of the Bible as our ground for believing in the authority of the Church. Of course, we do nothing of the kind. At this stage in the argument, we know nothing about the Bible being free from error; we are prepared to allow for the possibility (because the other man regards it as a possibility) that the Gospel record distorts, exaggerates, or even invents some of the facts. We are going to come to the Gospel narrative as if for the first time, without any prejudice or prepossession in its favour, and simply ask ourselves, What did the Hero of this narrative claim to be? And what proof did he offer us that this claim of his was justified?

VI

THE CLAIM

WE are to examine the question, what it was that our Lord claimed to be. The evidence we shall use is that of the Gospels, used simply as historical documents compiled by people who lived within a short lifetime of the events. I shall not use the fourth Gospel, because, as you will know if you read the letters in *The Times*, a lot of fantastic stuff is still talked about the date and authorship of that Gospel, so that if I used it I might seem to be begging the question. I say, "what our Lord claimed to be," namely, the Son of God in a unique sense. I do not intend to prove, what revelation itself teaches us, that he was the Second Person of the Blessed Trinity, that he united a human with a divine Nature under one Person, or that he came to make atonement for our sins. All that is beside our present point; our present business is to determine whether he claimed to be a fully-accredited ambassador from Almighty God, revealing the things of God to us; and that will be sufficiently established if we prove that he claimed to be the Son of God in a sense so intimate that it is impossible for any creature to share that title with him. If we prove that he *claimed* to be the Son of God, that does not as yet prove that he *was*. We have still to reckon with the possibility that he was deceived, or that he was deceiving us. We shall not have eliminated those possibilities until we have considered what credentials he offers for our inspection,

45

when he asks us to believe that his account of his own nature is true.

First, let us get this clear—that our Lord's identity was a mystery, to the men of his time no less than to those historians, not of our faith, who have written about his life since. And it was a mystery, you may say, of his own making. There was no doubt at all that he behaved and spoke like a prophet, to say the very least. He didn't set out to be a philosopher, appealing to human reason. Nor yet did he set out to be one of the scribes, that is one of the doctors of the Jewish church, handing on the tradition of the elders. He corrected the tradition of the elders; he was always saying "Moses told you this, but I tell you that," and when you think what the *ipse dixit* of Moses was and still is among the Jews you will realize what a break with tradition that was. One of the first impressions he made upon his audiences was that he taught them as one having authority, and not as their scribes. What sort of authority could that be? To the Jewish mind there was an obvious answer, he must be a prophet, like one of the Old Testament prophets. But, here again, he was a puzzle. The Old Testament prophets had never spoken in their own name. They always began their utterances with the rubric, "Thus saith the Lord"; or they would describe how they had seen a vision, how the Lord God of hosts had spoken to them, and how he had sent them to deliver a message from him. In our Lord's preaching there was never a word of all that. He spoke as one having authority, but the authority seemed somehow to belong to him personally, he never referred the credit of it elsewhere. And as he spoke, so he acted; he told devils to go out of men who were possessed without adjuring them by the name of God; he forgave sins, although the forgiveness of sins belonged to God only; he dispensed people from keeping the Sabbath; he cast the merchants out of the temple; he came into Jerusalem riding on an ass, in evident reference to an old prophecy which was always interpreted as describing the Messiah who was to come. He behaved, not as a prophet, but as something more than a prophet.

And all the time he keeps a finger on his lips. Everybody is asking, "Who is this? Isn't he the son of a carpenter? How did he learn letters? Can it be Elias come back to earth? Or one of the old prophets? Or is it a new prophet *like* them?" And he will not let any clue be given to the answer. When sick and blind are cured at his word, he charges them to tell no man; when the devils cry out that he is the Son of God, he solemnly adjures them to hold their peace. When he is asked by what authority he does these things, he puts off his questioners by asking them what they think about his predecessor, St John the Baptist; and they can say nothing, for they know that St John the Baptist pointed them to one who was even greater than himself. Again and again they test him with hard problems, to see if he will give away his secret, but always there is the same patient smile, the same impenetrable air of mystery.

Now, even if we had nothing more to go upon, this secrecy observed by our Lord would in itself be significant. I mean, people don't ordinarily bother about secrecy unless they have a secret to be kept. If you gave half a crown to a beggar, and he said, "God bless you, sir, you must be a saint," you would laugh and tell him not to be a fool. You wouldn't say, "Hush, don't mention it to anybody." If you were a government servant in Nigeria, and somebody asked you what authority you had to take taxes off him, you wouldn't ask him a riddle, and then when he gave it up say, "Well, I shan't tell you what authority I have to collect taxes either"; you would refer him to the Colonial Office. How you explain this policy on our Lord's part doesn't, for our present purposes, matter. I suppose the ordinary account we should give of it is that our

Lord did not want to put the faith of his contemporaries to too sudden a strain; he wanted to give them every chance of guessing who he was by gradually revealing himself, and didn't tell them in so many words until he saw that the right moment had come for it. But we aren't concerned with the explanation, only with the fact. And the fact of our Lord's silence about the origin of his mission seems to me enormously significant; if he had been an ordinary Rabbi, why not say he was a Rabbi? If he thought he was a prophet, why not say he was a prophet? A secret that is worth keeping has got to be a secret which is going to cause a sensation when it is found out.

However, our Lord wasn't content with mere silence. If you read the Gospels with a little attention, you will find that he was dropping out hints all the time, such as would lead on those who heard him to the conclusion that he was an ambassador from God, without saying so in so many words. Take, for example, his constant use of the title "Son of Man." It was probably a title connected in Jewish minds with the idea of the Messiah; and he himself talks freely about the day when the Son of Man will come in judgment. But I think he showed a preference for that title just because it emphasized his humanity; and what was the point of emphasizing his humanity unless he were something more than an ordinary human being? When Socrates assured his contemporaries that he really knew nothing, and was only asking questions because he wanted to learn from men wiser than himself, you can see at once he knew he was cleverer than they were. If you knew nothing about the Pope except that he called himself the slave of the slaves of God, you could infer quite easily that he regarded himself as the top man in Christendom, or he wouldn't have used such terms in describing himself. In the same way, you can give a good guess that our Lord wouldn't have been at such pains to call himself the Son of Man if he had not claimed to be something more than man when he did so.

Or again, take the way in which he refers to Almighty God. He very seldom talked about "God"—less than two dozen times altogether. What he does talk about is "the Father." And when we pray, he tells us that we are to begin our prayer with the phrase "Our Father." But how often do you find that phrase on his own lips? Never. He talks about "my Father" again and again; he talks about "your Father" again and again. But he never couples the two ideas together and talks about "our Father"—why? Because, clearly, he himself is the Son of God in one sense, those to whom he is speaking are sons of God in another. That is the sort of evidence which is all the more valuable because it is so unlikely that the evangelists—all four evangelists—should have observed that principle in all their records of our Lord's utterances, if they were not preserving an authentic tradition. How easy to have slipped into the phrase "our Father who is in heaven" accidentally, if they had been writing down legends!

The hints I have mentioned are negative ones; there are positive hints too. For example, when our Lord asks the Pharisees how the Messiah can be the Son of David, and yet David can call him "Lord," on the face of it he is just setting them a Rabbinical puzzle, but it's not hard to see that he is really challenging them to make up their minds about his own position. Or when Peter is asked whether he and his Master pay tribute, you remember the question our Lord puts to him, "From whom do earthly kings take tribute? From their own sons, or from strangers? From strangers—very well, then, the sons are free." But Peter will find the required coin in the mouth of the first fish which comes to his hook; "that take, and give it for me and for thee"—not "for us," but "for thee and for me"; for yourself, who *can* be expected to pay tribute, and for me, who owe nothing, because I am the Son of that God in whose honour the temple stands.

And the strongest hint of all, perhaps, was the parable of the Husbandmen, which comes at the very end of his ministry, just before the Passion, when the rulers of the Jews had already made up their minds to do away with him. The man who planted a vineyard was Almighty God, the husbandmen to whom he gave charge of it were the Jews themselves; so much they must have recognized immediately, for it was a figure familiar to them from their reading of the prophets. And it cannot have been difficult for them to recognize the way in which their fathers had treated the prophets, when they heard of the king's messengers being thrown out of the vineyard and put to death. "Last of all he sent unto them his son, for he said, They will reverence my son. But they said within themselves, This is the heir; come, let us kill him, that the inheritance may be ours." Imagine the feelings of a Pharisee listening to that parable! Could he have any doubt at all that the man who spoke those words was making himself the Son of God?

But even that, you see, was only a hint; there was nothing actionable about it; as far as we know, it was not even brought up at his trial. Were there no occasions, then, on which our Lord broke through this self-imposed silence and told men openly what he claimed to be? Yes, he did do that sometimes, and on three occasions specially. They are all familiar ones, but you will forgive me if I run through them this morning just to show you how definitely they complete the catena of evidence which we have been discussing. The first was when he had sent out his seventy disciples to preach, and they returned to tell him of the success of their mission. He does not speak *to* them; rather, it seems, he allows them to overhear him conversing with his heavenly Father. "O Father, Lord of heaven and earth, thou hast hid these things from the wise and prudent, and hast revealed them to little ones. Yea, Father, for so it hath seemed good in thy sight." And then, as if suddenly conscious that he has a human audience, he explains what his position is. "All things are delivered to me by my Father. And no one knoweth the Son, but the Father, neither doth anyone know the father but the son and he to whom it shall please the son to reveal him."

That, you see, is the exact statement we were waiting for. All things are delivered to me by my Father—a bad translation, as you so often get in our English Bible. *Omnia mihi tradita sunt*, all things have been handed on to me—there has been a *paradosis*, a *traditio*, from Father to Son. Just as some secret of family importance may be revealed to the heir by his father when he comes of age, so our Lord, incarnate on earth, has received from his heavenly Father a *tradition* which he is in a position to hand on to others, his earthly friends. And he intends to do so; no one knoweth the Father except the Son and he to whom it shall please the Son to reveal him —it is a *revelation*, in fact, which our Lord brings to men; a revelation about God; a revelation which none but he could make fully, since none but he knows the Father with the knowledge of perfect intimacy.

The second passage is too well known to need quoting at length; it is when, at Cæsarea Philippi, our Lord asks his apostles what is the current opinion of men about him; and when these have been mentioned, he asks what is *their* opinion of him. And Peter answers, Thou art the Christ, the Son of the living God. "Blessed art thou, Simon son of John," our Lord says, "because flesh and blood [that is, human wisdom] hath not revealed it to thee, but my Father who is in heaven." This is the completion, you see, of the passage we have just been discussing; no one knows the Father, except through revelation from the Son; and nobody, it seems, knows the Son except through revelation from the

Father—like Peter, who is to be the rock of the new covenant. But the important thing is that here our Lord, although he forbids his apostles to tell what they have heard, does nevertheless accept, formally, the title of Messiah, and there is no secrecy between him and his friends about it any longer.

Was it only to his friends, then, that he admitted who he was? No, to his enemies too; but only when their agreed determination to crucify him had made it unnecessary to spare their feelings any longer. The high priest, at his trial, adjures him by the divine name to say whether or no he is the Christ, the Son of the living God. And he answers openly, "I am." Now, observe how impossible it is to take this as anything but a confession of his most intimate convictions about himself. He was on oath; to accept the statement in any false sense was perjury. He was being tried for his life, and the answer he gave meant certain death; he could have saved himself by withholding it. They were plunging into the guilt of shedding innocent blood; and he was abetting them, if he accepted the title loosely, recklessly, without supplying necessary qualifications. If, then, when he called himself the Son of God, he meant no more than that he was a man like themselves, but distinguished from themselves by the enjoyment, in a unique degree, of prophetic gifts, why did he not say so? Is it credible that he should *not* have said so, when he knew that the alternative was a charge of blasphemy from which he could not defend himself?

Well, I haven't nearly been able to exhaust the arguments it would be possible to bring forward on this subject. I haven't said anything, for example, about the way in which our Lord habitually talks of the supernatural world as if he were familiar with all its details—how he seems to know all about God's methods in the ordering of Providence, all about the holy angels and the service they do, about the devils and the power they have, about the circumstances of the last judgment, and the conditions of life in a future state. And all that, mark you, without ever quoting his authority for the statements he makes; simply letting drop these references to the unseen world as it were absent-mindedly, as if he didn't realize that people might turn upon him and ask him the question, "How do you know?" That attitude, as an ordinary matter of human psychology, is not the common attitude of the impostor; the impostor is always on the look-out for such criticisms, and careful to explain what the source of his knowledge was. It is not altogether unlike the attitude of a lunatic, suffering from hallucinations; but again, as a matter of abnormal human psychology, you would expect such a lunatic to be continually dwelling on his obsessions, never able to talk about anything else; whereas in our Lord's teaching these references are only occasional, only incidental.

I've been trying to show that our Lord did *claim* to bring with him a unique revelation from God—not merely a new moral code, but the foundations of a theological certitude which previous ages had never even aspired to. And that is the conclusion which would, I think, be reached by any impartial critic approaching the documents for the first time. The reason why many non-Catholic writers, especially of the older generation, are blind to all that, don't recognize the far-reaching nature of our Lord's claims, is because they shrink from the corollaries which such a recognition would involve. They shrink, through a kind of rationalist prejudice, from having to admit that our Lord was, in a unique sense, the Son of God. They shrink, through a kind of sentimental reverence, from having to admit that one whose career has had so profound an influence on history was an impostor or a madman. But it is a mark of intellectual cowardice, to shrink from corollaries. God wouldn't have given us an intellect, if he didn't want us to think straight.

VII

EARLY IN THE MORNING

ABOUT the year A.D. 60, a prisoner stood before the tribunal of Porcius Festus, the Roman governor of Judæa. By the side of Festus sat King Herod Agrippa the Second, a subject prince who governed most of the country to the north and east of Judæa. And the prisoner, in the course of his statement, referred to the remarkable fulfilment of Old Testament prophecy which took place when a man in Jerusalem rose from the dead, about twenty-seven years before. Festus, a newcomer to the province, said, "My dear fellow, you must be mad." And the prisoner, St Paul, turned to King Herod, and said, "The king here knows that I'm talking sense when I say that. For I am persuaded that these things are not hidden from him. For these things were not done in a corner." Herod was not an old man, only about thirty-three, and the event in question belonged to the time when he was about six. St Paul appeals, either to his boyish memories of what he heard at the time, or to the tradition of local history in which he was brought up. In either case, he treats the Resurrection of our Lord as a known fact. All he labours to show is that the fact proves our Lord's Divinity.

Yes, you say, but twenty-seven years is rather a long time-lag, and the stories one hears in the nursery are sometimes rather exaggerated. Very well, then, let us go back to an earlier scene, also recorded in the Acts of the Apostles; and to a speech, made this time by St Peter—those speeches in the Acts, nearly any critic will agree, have the stamp of authenticity about them, even if they were only written up afterwards from notes. It was the Day of Pentecost, a great feast of the Jews; and St Peter stood in the street addressing a crowd of Jews who had come there to worship—many from foreign parts, but the bulk of them, we must suppose, residents in the city itself. He recalls to them a passage in the Psalms, where David says, "Thou, O God, wilt not leave my soul in hell, neither wilt thou suffer thy holy one to see corruption." Who, he asks, is this Holy One referred to? King David himself? No, King David *did* see corruption; we all know where his tomb is. Therefore it must refer to Jesus of Nazareth, who rose from the grave and did *not* see corruption. Now, St Peter was talking exactly fifty days after the alleged event. The tomb of Jesus Christ was there, close to Jerusalem; about as far off, say, as Somerville is from here. And he challenges them to go and look for the Body of Jesus of Nazareth there. Or rather, he doesn't, because the mystery of its disappearance is on all men's lips. He does not prove the doctrine of the Empty Tomb; he refers to it as a fact and bases his whole argument on it. No; these things were not done in a corner. What had happened?

On either March 20 or March 27, rather more than nineteen hundred years ago, it seems that a handful of soldiers, probably Roman soldiers, were on guard outside a tomb on the outskirts of Jerusalem. The tomb was freshly made, but it had been diverted from its original purpose, whatever that was. The body of a Galilean Teacher, who had been crucified by the Roman governor's orders, had been hastily put there two days before. No more elaborate funeral had been possible at the time, because it was the Paschal sabbath, and no manual work might be done. Two Jewish gentlemen had carried out

3

this burial, apparently by themselves; but their action had been witnessed by some women, who were followers of the dead Prophet. A very heavy stone had been rolled against the door of the tomb, which was carved out of the natural rock; a stone light enough for two men to put in position, but too heavy for five women to move out of its position again. It was a natural precaution, at a time and in a country where robbing of graves was not unknown. But the soldiers were posted there as a very special precaution; because some words used by the dead man, not long before, had suggested to the authorities that he believed himself capable of rising again from the tomb.

As events turned out, the precaution was of no great value. Early in the morning an earthquake shock, the second in two days, was felt in Jerusalem; and it may be that, through some fault in the ground, it was felt with especial violence just where the tomb was. (We read in the papers last week that the Church of the Holy Sepulchre, raised long afterwards on this site, has just been closed for repairs, because an earthquake which took place last October has damaged the structure.) The soldiers came back to the city in alarm; and some of them made a report to those who had given them their orders. The report was, that when the shock was felt the stone had rolled away from the door of the sepulchre, and an angel had appeared to them, sitting on the stone, dazzling white in the uncertain light of very early dawn. We do not know whether the Jewish authorities believed this story; but they held it was the part of prudence to hush the matter up, and bribed the soldiers to say that they had fallen asleep, and that while they were asleep the body of the Galilean prophet had been stolen away by his disciples. It has been pointed out long ago that their story was not very cleverly concocted; for if the soldiers were really asleep, how could they tell who had stolen the body, or whether it had been stolen at all? But it was the best that could be managed; and this story was still current among the Jews, it appears, years afterwards. The gospel which tells us all this was probably, unlike the other gospels, written in Judæa; and it may well have preserved the inner history, long kept secret, of what the soldiers saw, and why, at dawn, the tomb was left unguarded.

Unguarded it evidently was. It must have been quite soon after the soldiers left that some five women came to visit the tomb and anoint the body, a tribute which they had not been able to pay on the Friday evening. It was still dark, but only with the dusk of twilight; they would not have left the city in pitch darkness. They were expecting to have difficulty about moving the stone; and their first surprise was when they, too, found it rolled away from its place. One of the women, and perhaps the most active spirit among them, she whom we call Mary Magdalen, was so much excited or alarmed by this that she went back at once to report the occurrence to the dead man's disciples. The rest of the women, however, remained at the tomb, and saw very much more. What was it they saw?

They reported afterwards, like the soldiers, that they had had a "vision of angels." Two men stood by them in shining garments and, this time, had speech with them. To be more accurate, it looks as if one of the two had been outside the tomb, where the soldiers had seen him earlier, while the other was inside, and not visible till you had entered. The evidence on these points of detail is not exactly clear. True evidence very seldom is. Bribe a handful of soldiers, and they will spread the same lie all over Jerusalem. Take three women to the tomb, none of them expecting to find anything unusual, and you will have to piece the story together for yourself. One will have seen two angels, another can only swear to the presence of a single angel; this witness was conscious of the angel first and the empty tomb afterwards, that one will have got the order of her impressions confused. But their evidence is quite clear in its main outlines; whether of their own accord or because the angels invited them to do so, they went into the tomb, looked for the body, and found that it was not there.

The angels had given them a message; they were to tell the disciples of the dead Prophet that he had risen from the dead, and that they were to go back to Galilee, the part of the country to which they belonged; there, far away from the scene of these recent disturbances, they would meet him again. The women hastened away on this errand, and said nothing to anybody on the way. Why is this detail mentioned? Probably because, on the way, they met two of the disciples in question, without accosting them. By now, you see, Mary Magdalen will have reached Jerusalem, with her story that the grave-door was lying open—so far, that is all the news she has. Two of the disciples, Peter and John, set out, running, to verify the truth of her statement; their first thought may have been that the tomb had been robbed. But if they passed, on their way, the rest of the women, no conversation was exchanged between them; that is the point. They came to the sepulchre not knowing what they were to find there, except that the stone would be rolled away. Mary Magdalen followed the two disciples, presumably at a distance.

One of the two disciples, John, has left us his own story of the event. Both he and Peter went into the tomb, and verified the absence of the body. They noticed something else; still more remarkable. The body had been wrapped in a winding-sheet, and a napkin had been wound round the head. These were found, apparently, still in position, as if the body had passed through them without disturbing them. John tells us that the sight was enough to carry conviction to his own mind; from that moment he believed that he who was dead had risen again. No angels appeared to them, and they went back as they had come.

So far, it will be noticed, the direct evidence about the body of Jesus of Nazareth is purely negative; you have the consistent story of a disappearance, but no story of an appearance. And so far, it is well to observe, the evidence never seems to have been refuted, or even contradicted. We have seen what was the official story put about in Jerusalem; it tried to provide an explanation of the disappearance, as if the fact were beyond denial. So it was that, fifty days afterwards, one of the dead man's disciples made a speech before a large crowd of people in Jerusalem itself, and treated the fact of the empty tomb as a generally admitted fact on which you could base your arguments. And years later, Paul of Tarsus, on his trial before King Herod Agrippa, shows the same confidence. He is persuaded, he says, that the events about which he has been talking—they included the Resurrection—are well known to the king; "for these things were not done in a corner."

But we hear no more in our records about the negative evidence, because at this point the positive evidence begins. Mary Magdalen stood by the tomb weeping after the two disciples had gone; weeping, because she evidently thought that somebody had taken her Master's body away. It might be the authorities, it might be his enemies, it might be common robbers—it did not matter to her. She has come out with her ointments to do honour to the dead man's memory, and now it is too late; that is all she thinks about. She looks into the tomb (for the first time, apparently), and sees an angel sitting there, as the other women had, some minutes back. Before she has time to answer the angel's mysterious greeting, a shadow (I suppose) passes over the door; she looks round, and sees somebody standing beside her. Perhaps it will be the gardener; she will ask if he knows anything about her loss. And the rest of the story is told in two words of dialogue: "Mary . . . Master!" In such a short compass is the script of the world's greatest drama comprised.

The other women will by now have been on their return journey to the tomb, after delivering their message. Perhaps by this time they had rejoined Mary Magdalen, and shared her experience; if not, it must have been soon afterwards that they, too, met their risen Master and clung to his feet. These first rumours of an appearance were not believed by the other disciples, who waited for confirmation of the news. And it was not till the evening or late afternoon that it came. The dead Prophet appeared, living, to Peter, that one of his disciples whom he had appointed to be the leader of the others, strengthening their faith. Curiously, no details have been preserved to us of this interview. But Peter described it, fourteen or fifteen years afterwards, to Paul of Tarsus; and Paul of Tarsus, writing ten years later again to the Christians in Corinth, refers to it as if it were an important plank in the platform he used, when he preached the Gospel message.

It must have been shortly before or shortly after this that he, whose body men looked for vainly in the sepulchre, appeared again to two of his followers, as they were walking out to a village seven or eight miles from Jerusalem. For whatever reason, they did not recognize him till the very last moment, although he walked for some way with them and shared their evening meal. Like Mary Magdalen, they found a difficulty in recognizing him. Why, we do not know; but do not let us be told that the appearance was, therefore, a hallucination. It was as far as possible the exact opposite. A hallucination makes us mistake a stranger for a friend; this inhibition of which we are speaking, whatever it was, made people mistake, at first, their Friend for a stranger. The two disciples went back to Jerusalem to the upper room in which, as usual, the followers of the Crucified were assembled; the doors were locked, for fear of hostile action by the Jewish authorities. While they were describing their experience, the Master himself appeared suddenly in their midst; quieted their fears; ate and drank with them to convince them that it was no mere phantom shape they saw.

Those are the events of the first Easter Day, collected from six different sources, of which all except one seem to have been compiled in their present shape within forty years of the events which they described. What are we going to make of them? We are the jury, as it were, which must sit in inquest, age after age, on the events recorded; and yet, are we the jury, or is it we who are on our trial? Anyhow, the Christian submission is this—that the events I have described, coupled with a set of similar events spread over a period of forty days, coupled with the inferences which we may draw from the behaviour of the dead Prophet's followers, immediately afterwards, coupled with a living tradition which has been handed down, from that century to this, by a body of men singularly tenacious of tradition, establishes the supernatural character of the Mission with which Jesus of Nazareth went about the world nineteen hundred years ago. If you dissent from that finding, then it is for you to decide at what point you will dissent from it. Will you doubt the authenticity of the documents? Or the veracity of their authors? Or the good faith of the witnesses on whom those authors relied? Or, if you do not doubt the facts themselves, will you doubt the philosophical construction which has been put upon the facts?

I cannot try to meet all those positions. I am only concerned now to challenge one of them; to meet the contentions of the people who say, "Oh, yes, there is no doubt the documents are authentic; no doubt that those who compiled them were, in the main, conscientious; no doubt that the witnesses on whom they depended, simple people and evidently people of good will, were doing their best to describe what they heard and saw. Only, of course, there must be some mistake, because miracles don't happen." There must be some mistake; yes, no doubt. Only, what mistake can it possibly have been?

Take the story of the empty tomb by itself. Could you have circumstantial evidence more complete? The body had disappeared; is there any possible motive to assign for its removal by any human agent using natural means? There is absolutely none. Even if you refuse to believe that the Jews took special precautions to keep the tomb safe, you must still recognize that the story of their doing so is true to life. It was in their interest to keep the body, and to be able at any moment to produce it, should any claim be made that Jesus of Nazareth had risen from the dead. If they removed it from the grave, why did they not produce it afterwards? Nor had Pilate, the Roman governor, any reason for wishing to smuggle away the body of the man he had crucified; its presence might conceivably lead to rioting and disturbance, but its disappearance was far more likely to have that effect. The women cannot have stolen it, for they were not strong enough to move away the stone, let alone to overpower a military guard. Did the guard, then, desert their posts, and some other human agent remove the body before the women came? That was the only possibility which presented itself to Mary Magdalen. Could Joseph of Arimathea have carried it away, or Nicodemus? But, in any of these events, why did not the agent who had removed the body give any sign, afterwards, of what he had done? If he were friendly disposed towards the disciples, to the disciples; if he were ill disposed, to the Jews? And, whatever their motives, why did they leave the winding-sheet and the napkin lying there, instead of taking the body as it lay? The presence of the grave-clothes is also fatal to the theory, which has (I believe) been suggested, that the body was buried deeper in the ground as the result of the earthquake.

No, if you are going to give a merely natural account of the whole story, the account which was first given still holds the field. I mean, that there was deliberate fraud on the part of the disciples, who wanted to give the impression that their Master had risen from the dead. What you have to decide is, whether such a notion is consistent with the behaviour of those same people two days before, at the Crucifixion, running away and leaving their Master to face his persecutors alone, and with the behaviour of those same people, in the years which followed, suffering imprisonment and dying in support of a story which they had made up to deceive the public. I wonder, did they?

VIII

EGYPTIAN ENCHANTMENTS

IF any of you has ever tried arguing about miracles with his non-Catholic friends he has probably had a disconcerting experience. After you have spent half the evening trying to refute the objections of a man who says that miracles are simply impossible, and that there is no serious evidence that any such event has ever occurred in human history, somebody else chips in on the other side of the argument; and you have to spend the other half of the evening answering the objections of a man who says, of course, there have been miracles in human history, some of them done by Christians, but why make such a fuss about it? All religions can produce their miracles, just as much as ours; they were all cradled in an atmosphere of supernatural happenings. And, more than that, there are religions which can produce miracles to-day; the Christian Scientists with their faith-healing cures, the spiritualists with their extraordinary revelations of secrets which could not have been known to the medium, their photographs of preternatural bodies, and all the rest of it. Not to mention the odd people you read of in the papers, the dervishes who can walk on hot coals without burning themselves, or the man who is, I believe, on view now, who is said to be able to emit a luminous radiance from his body whenever he sets his mind to it. All that, your friend will say, has to be taken into account before you use the evidence of miracles to prove, or even help to prove, the truth of Christianity or of Catholicism. You have done more, you have proved the truth of all religions, or practically all religions, while you were about it.

That's always happening to one in religious discussions. You start out by having to show that miracles are not impossible; and before you know where you are you are having to answer the objection that they are ridiculously common. In a word, to round off our course, we want to consider the question, "Does anybody else besides God do miracles?" What are we to make of miracles outside the Church? Do the Mahomedan miracles prove Mahomedanism? Did the Jansenist miracles prove Jansenism? Do the Christian Scientist miracles prove Christian Science? And it's quite important, you know, because the English people at its roots is curiously superstitious, and there is a reaction, nowadays, from the confident scepticism of our fathers. We want to have an attitude towards the people who are too positive, not only towards the people who are too negative.

In the first place, let us get our minds clear about the statement that all religions are cradled in stories of miracle. It is quite true that when men are writing of a very distant past, and concerned to honour the memory of some great hero, or even to record the origins of their gods, they do tend to weave into their account wonderful happenings—after all, it all happened a very long time ago, and things must have been very different. That is one thing; but, you see, the Christian religion is in quite a different case. The miracles related of our Lord and his apostles are related by eye-witnesses, or at least by contemporaries; the documents in which they occur are documents whose date can be established, beyond the possibility of reasonable cavil, as going back behind the destruction of Jerusalem in A.D. 70. And the miracles are bound up, structurally, with the narrative; you cannot, with whatever ingenuity, separate the documents into different strata, the earlier of which will be non-miraculous. It is extraordinary the way people will tell you that they believe the Gospel, but not the Gospel miracles. If you ask them what they mean by the Gospel, they will tell you that there was a man called Jesus of Nazareth who went about doing good. When they say that, bring them up short by asking them what good he did? Oh, he was gentle, he was considerate, he was forgiving. But where do you hear that he ever gave money to the poor, or nursed the sick, or comforted the mourner, or buried the dead, or visited anybody in prison? Nowhere; he may have, but the Gospels tell us nothing about it. When we say that our Lord went about doing good, we mean that he healed the sick, raised the dead, and so on; that very habit of "doing good" which is the first thought the mention of our Lord's name calls up to us, is, when you come to think of it, a habit of performing miracles. You can't get on without the miracles; the whole story goes to pieces.

No, the appearance of Christianity is accompanied by something which did not really belong to the world in which it appeared. A belief in miracles; an expectation that miracles would take place, a conviction that they had taken place, on such and such occasions. When our Lord sends out his apostles he tells them to perform miracles, to lay their hands on the sick, and drink poison without fear of harm. Now, it is perfect nonsense to talk, though you will hear people some-times talk, as if the men of that day found it easy to believe in miracles because they weren't such frightfully scientific people as we are nowadays. Oh, it is true that common people were superstitious, believed in fortune-telling and in love-philtres and witchcraft generally. So you will find Simon Magus all the rage at Samaria, and the governor of Cyprus keeping a sort of tame soothsayer, and so on. But people were not expecting miracles all the time, and when they saw the miracles done by the apostles their reactions showed it. When St Paul healed the crippled man at Lystra, they all said, "The gods are come down to us in the likeness of man," and tried to do sacrifice to them. So, when St Paul was uninjured by the bite of the snake, the people of Malta thought he was a god. They did not look upon a miracle as something ordinary or commonplace; it carried their minds straight back to their mythologies, to the stories of Philemon and Baucis, or the invulnerable Achilles.

Another difference I think you can notice between the tall stories you will find recorded in the classical writers and the miracles of our Lord. Most of the tall stories you will find in the classical writers are stories of omens and portents, or of punishments inflicted by the gods on people who had defied them. The characteristic of nearly all our Lord's miracles, nearly all those in the Acts of the Apostles, nearly all those in the lives of the saints, is that they were designed to show, not God's power only, but also his mercy. It is to heal the sick, to comfort the bereaved, to relieve the poor, to deliver the unjustly imprisoned, to save those in imminent danger of death, that the Christian miracles for the most part were performed. God wants us to see that he is powerful, but he wants us to see that he is merciful too. Apart from the Old Testament, in which our Lord's coming and character were foreshadowed, you will not find, or will very seldom find, those miracles of mercy in the records of antiquity. I think it is probably true to say that the Christian miracles have set the type, and have produced the impetus, for most of the stories of religious miracle which have cropped up since then. It is curious to note that the consciousness of Christianity as a rival seems to have the effect of making other religions breed stories of miracle for themselves. I think there cannot really be much doubt that Philostratus' life of Apollonius of Tyana, written in the third century A.D., was a Pagan come-back deliberately designed to meet the overwhelming competition of Christian teaching. I understand it is true to say that the earliest lives of Buddha have no miraculous element in them, and that stories like that which represent him as born of a virgin date from a time when Christianity had already penetrated into India. And, as Paley pointed out, the miracles attributed to Mahomet are not recorded in the Koran—Mahomet himself seems to have made rather a point of the idea that miracles were unnecessary—but only came into circulation several centuries later, when Christendom and Islam were already matched in the struggle for world-domination. If all religions have their miracles, you see, that does not prove that there may not have been a certain infringement of copyright.

And, of course, as these conferences have insisted, the Catholic religion differs from most other religions, differs even from most other denominations of Christianity, in that it was not merely cradled in an atmosphere of the miraculous, but lives and breathes in an atmosphere of the miraculous. Miracles are not always equally abundant, but the faith is always there; when the deacon Peter asks St Gregory in his dialogues why it is that miracles don't happen nowadays, St Gregory first of all gives reasons why they shouldn't happen, and then points out that they do. All the discoveries of science about the nature of diseases and so on have not lessened our faith in the possibility of miracle; rather, they have increased it. For, in proportion as medicine grows more exact in its methods and more careful in its habits of observation, in that proportion we can feel more certain, when such and such a cure is effected, that the finger of God was really there. When you hear doctors doubting about the miracles at Lourdes, you will find that the complaint they are making is not one against religion; diagnosis, they say; some ass of a French G.P. didn't know his own business. If that is so, we can only hope that doctors will get more and more scientific; then the miracles at Lourdes will be more manifest than ever.

Meanwhile, what are we going to make of these miracles outside the Church, or strange happenings anyhow outside the Church, which have taken place in recent times or are taking place now, among the Christian Scientists, among the spiritualists, in odd cases which crop up here and there of dual personality, of queer pathological states, and so on? In the first place, let us take a leaf out of our opponents' book—I mean, the book which they have just put back in its shelf, the anti-miraculous book—and admit quite freely that there may, probably enough, be powers in the mind to influence matter which are still unexplored, and perhaps may be incapable of scientific analysis, and yet do not pass the bounds of the natural. I was being told the other day of an experiment at which Dr Schiller was present, when a medium, apparently by simply looking at a piece of paper, managed to reproduce on it an exact facsimile of a well-known criminal's thumb-mark; the criminal was dead, but they had a copy of the thumb-mark in the police records. Well, there are people who will say, "Doesn't that prove that there is a life after death?" To my mind, it doesn't prove anything of the kind. If the spirit of the criminal was really there at the seance, I don't see why it should want to go leaving its thumb-marks about all over the place, even if it had a thumb to leave marks with. If it retained any of the characteristics it had during life, I should have thought its first instinct would have been to wear gloves. No, if you assume that the facts are as reported, and that there was really no trickery, then I should say without hesitation that it shows we have only begun to understand the least little bit about thought-transference. And in the same way I would say of the Christian Scientists that, if their results are really genuine, then it shows that will-power can do more in the way of interference with matter than we thought it could; just as, according to some stories one hears, it can enable men to stick knives into themselves without bleeding, or walk on hot iron without being scorched.

Of course that means, and we have got to recognize that it means, a certain modification on our part of the claims which our forefathers have been accustomed to make when the question of the miraculous was discussed. It means that the total number of ascertainable miracles with which the records of sanctity have hitherto been credited is somewhat reduced. For instance, I had speech, last July, with a woman at Lourdes, a Protestant woman from Chorley in Lancashire, who was, that afternoon, enjoying the use of her sight for the first time in, I think, twenty months. It had been restored to her suddenly during the great procession of the Host in the afternoon. Now, that may have been a miracle. It was certainly a great favour, and I hope the woman has become a Catholic by now. But those who were in charge of the hospital did not even trouble to report the case to the Bureau des Constatations —why? Because there had never been anything wrong with the physical organ of sight; the woman had been unable to see because she could not, or thought she could not, open her eyelids. And that, you see, may have been a merely hysterical condition. I think it is established by now that hysterical patients can sometimes be cured by a sudden shock of any kind, like the son of Croesus in Herodotus who had always been dumb, but suddenly broke into speech when his father's capital was being sacked by the enemy. So in this case; there is always the possibility of a miracle, but the circumstances were such that you could not appeal to it as a miracle for evidential purposes; it may equally well have been a cure of hysteria by shock. We should have heard plenty about it in the papers if it happened in England. But when those things happen at Lourdes, so common are they, they are not even reported to the Bureau.

But, of course, when we have said that, the objector will try to press his advantage. If you admit, he says, that some of the cures at your holy places are due to mind-healing or shock, and admit in the same breath that we do not as yet know how far the triumphs of mind over matter may not go, without passing beyond the natural order, surely we have a right to extend the same principle, and make it cover ALL the stories of remarkable cures, whether at Lourdes or elsewhere? Surely the difference between major and minor miracles is not a difference of kind, but of degree; and we shall be able to explain the major as well as the minor when we have investigated the natural possibilities more thoroughly? Well, the debating answer to that is that we wish they would hurry up and do it. These men of science, many of them actuated by fanatical hatred against the Church, have had the opportunity of producing hypnotic cures to rival the cures of Lourdes these eighty years past, and they have failed to do it, certainly not from lack of good-will. But the answer is better expressed thus. It is grossly unscientific to assume that because you have an explanation which will admittedly cover some of a group of phenomena, therefore the same explanation, by parity of reasoning, MUST cover the whole. There is such a thing as suggestion in medicine. Most of you will remember the old *Punch* picture of the doctor taking out the thermometer from a patient's mouth, and the patient saying, "Ah, doctor, that done me a power of good." I imagine it happens fairly frequently that a doctor pretends to give a sick person a sleeping-draught, which in reality is just water with a little colouring matter, and the patient obediently goes to sleep through the power of suggestion; or the doctor pretends to inject morphia and really injects nothing of the kind, with the same result. Does that prove that *all* sleeping-draughts really work through the power of suggestion; that real morphia has no powers, except those with which it plays upon the patient's suggestibility? No, until they have paralleled our major miracles, or conclusively disproved the evidence for them, the least science can do is to say, "We have explained a certain proportion of these cures by mind-healing; the remainder seem due to another cause, which we have not yet identified."

When we say that, of course, all the other miracle-mongers are up in arms. How is it, they ask, that you Catholics expect scientists to take notice of your miracles, and submit them to patient investigation, while you yourselves will not investigate the cures worked by Christian Science, or join a spiritualist circle to find out for yourselves whether extraordinary things really do happen there? Our answer to that objection is perfectly simple. It is that we do not know and perhaps do not greatly care whether such things can be explained by natural causes or whether they take their origin from spiritual agencies which are not of God. All we know is that such modern miracles do not conform to the type of miracles with which, as we believe, the Christian message has always been associated; that they are not such as can be reconciled with the Nature of God and the character of his dealings with mankind, as we know them either by reason or by revelation. That point I must expand quite briefly.

The divine miracles, as we understand them, are exceptional favours, bestowed here and there, now and then—birthday presents, as it were, to remind us that we are after all his children. He does not perform them as a rule to order, unfailingly, in answer to some special effort on our part. There are exceptions to that rule; the blood-miracles of Naples and the surrounding country for example, if they are miracles indeed. But in the ordinary way he does mean miracles to be the exception, not the rule. We are not to pension off the doctors and neglect to have the drains seen to because, sometimes, there may have been a miraculous cure of typhoid. We are not to neglect prayers for the dead because, now and again, we have supernatural proof that a soul has missed its Purgatory. That is what is the trouble with these modern devotees of miracle; they overdo it; they make it the rule, not the exception. They want us to believe that there is no such thing as pain, that it cannot be God's will for a human being to suffer. They want us to believe that there is no such thing as death, no plunge into the mysteries of the unknown. And that is not our philosophy, nor is it a human philosophy at all; we cannot believe that God countenances it, whatever manifestations may accompany it.

IX

THE LIVING WITNESS

HERE are people who call themselves Christians, without belonging to any religious organization. Granted that the full revelation of God is to be found in our Lord Jesus Christ, we must still prove, before considering the nature of his Church, that he did found a Church at all; that he did want an assemblage of people, inheriting all down the centuries the same tradition of doctrine, to continue the work of his revelation and to safeguard its genuineness. That point I want to make this morning, in as short a space as I can manage.

Any alleged revelation from God to man must, if its influence is to last beyond the lifetime of men contemporary with its appearance, perpetuate itself in one or other of two ways. Its doctrine must be enshrined either in a book or in a legitimately constituted succession of living teachers. You can point to many religions of the book in the course of history; take Mormonism, for example. Mormonism was founded by a young American called Joseph Smith, who declared that he had found a book made entirely of plates of thin gold, hidden in the side of a hill near his home; it was said to have been written in "reformed Egyptian," whatever that may be, and it contained a full history of the colonization of North America after the destruction of the tower of Babel. Eight persons swore that they had seen the gold-plate original; but all that survived was a translation made by some of Smith's friends, Smith himself dictating it to them from behind a curtain. It was round this Book of Mormon that the whole cult grew up; the gold plates themselves were conveniently carried off by an angel before anyone else saw them.

But there is this trouble about any religion whose revelation is merely enshrined in a book; that doubts of interpretation may arise as to what the book means, and then you have no means of knowing which is the right and which is the wrong interpretation. Or new conditions arise, and it is necessary for the new sect to have an attitude and a policy about them; yet it is in vain that they go to the book for guidance. So that even a religion which starts from a book tends more and more to grow into a church; to develop its own rulers and its own system of government; to live by traditions which are handed on, not merely by what is found written in the book from which it started. That happened, of course, with the Mormons; the Book of Mormon said distinctly that each believer was only to have one wife, but this arrangement was found inconvenient, and after a private revelation given to Joseph Smith was discontinued.

Well, as you know, the Christian religion is not and never has been the religion of a book. It was perfectly easy for our Lord Jesus Christ, if he had wanted to, to have dictated to his Apostles a book as long as the Old Testament or as the Koran, and to have left this book, after his Ascension, to guide all the world into his truth. But he didn't do that; and for a score of years, perhaps, after his Ascension, the Christian religion was preached everywhere by word of mouth; nobody studied the Gospels or preached about the Gospels, because there were no Gospels to study or to preach about. It was only when living memories began to fade that there was a demand for authentic accounts of our Lord's own words, so far as they could be remembered; our Lord's own actions, so far as they were not already familiar to the faithful. No, our Lord did not leave a book, he left behind him a body of people. That, after all, was natural. He came to fulfil the old prophecies of the Jews; and their prophets had told them that when the Messiah came he would save a remnant of the people; not all the people, but a faithful remnant of them. This remnant our Lord usually referred to as a kingdom, the kingdom of God, the kingdom of heaven. On two occasions at least he called it his congregation or assembly; and the Greek word for that, *ecclesia*, is, of course, the word by which we know it, his Church. That became, from the first ages, its common appellation; you will find the term used no less than fifty times in the writings of St Paul. Of course, it was to be something more than the mere word "kingdom" implies; our Lord told his followers that he was the Vine and they were the branches, that is, that there was a spiritual unity which was to bind each of them to the others and all of them to him. He told them that the Holy Spirit was to come and dwell in them, to guide them into all truth. But the point to notice here is that, deliberately, he left behind him a Church.

Everybody who has studied the Gospels seriously admits that; all Christians, you may say roughly, admit that. But then, what kind of fact is this Church, of which he speaks in such glowing terms, to which he makes such glorious promises? Is it a definite body of people, united together by external marks, by a common worship and a common faith, with its own definite boundaries, so that you can say with certainty So-and-so is a member of the Church, So-and-so does not belong to the Church? The contrary has often been held by Protestant thinkers, and is still at the back of a great deal of Protestant thought. The true-blue Protestant idea of the Church is that it is not a definite body of people to which you can point, whose numbers you can count. It is the total number of those souls which will, as a matter of fact, be saved and find their way to heaven. Only God knows the number of those souls, and which they are; here on earth we have our sects and our denominations, but no one of these, nor even the sum total of these, can be described as the Church of Christ. The Church of Christ is something invisible, a hidden body, which will never be known until the day of judgment. Of course, if that doctrine were true, it would be merely wasting your time to give you conferences all through this term about the marks of the true Church; the whole point of the true Church, on this theory, is that there are no marks by which it can possibly be recognized. No external organization, in faith or discipline or worship, can give you any idea of its extent. Even the old lady—you have probably heard the story—who founded a particular sect of her own, to which only two people belonged, herself and her coachman, felt that difficulty. When they asked whether she really believed that she and her coachman were the only people who would ever get to heaven, she replied, "Weel, I'm no so sure about John."

It's worth while, then, to look a little at our Lord's teaching and try to find out what kind of thing he meant this Church of his to be. Was it to be an invisible Church, such as the old-fashioned Protestants declared it to be, or is it a visible fact, so that we can point to it and define it, and say that it numbers so many souls in China, or in Lancashire, or wherever it may be, without fear of contradiction?

The sentence in which our Lord settled that question, it seems to me, once for all, is a sentence which he used not once but several times, so that it is familiar to all of us—I mean the sentence, "Many are called, but few are chosen." I'm sorry to bother you with Greek, but there's no help for it here; the word *ecclesia* does mean something called out, that and nothing else. The Church, then, the *ecclesia*, consists of the *kletoi*, the people who are called; and less than a hundred per cent. of these (that is all "few" means) are chosen; that is to say, will be rewarded with eternal life in heaven. All through his parables our Lord is rubbing that lesson in. The kingdom of heaven, the Church, is like ten virgins, five wise and five foolish—only five of them are saved, but all ten of them are in the Church. The kingdom of heaven is like a great supper, to which a number of people are called, but one of them is found to be without a wedding garment, and is cast out into the exterior darkness. It is like a net thrown into the sea, which brings in some fish that are eatable, and some that are worthless; it is like a field, in which some of the crop is honest wheat, and the rest mere useless cockle. Now, when our Lord goes out of his way to talk like that, does he not make it clear that his Church is something different from that ideal assembly of the elect which the old-fashioned Protestants declared it to be? Does he not make it clear that it consists of a recognizable body of people, some of whom, but not all of whom, will attain everlasting life?

Our Lord did more than found a Church; he founded a hierarchy. Of course, one expects any religious teacher to have his own group of chosen disciples; a few who go about with him everywhere and see more of him than the generality of his contemporaries do. But if you come to think of it, all through the record which the Gospels give us our Lord is more concerned with the instruction of twelve men than with all the rest of the Jews. He must teach the multitudes and heal their sick, because they will not leave him alone; but when he sees the chance, he will steal away into a desert place with his disciples. And after his Resurrection, though we are told that on one occasion he appeared to more than 500 brethren at once, it is evident that for the most part he was closeted with his twelve apostles, speaking to them of the things which pertain to the kingdom of God, that is, his

Church. They were not, then, merely witnesses whom he must always have about him, they were something more important than that; the nucleus round which his Church was to grow. And so it is to them he speaks in words such as he never uses in his public discourses: "As the Father hath sent me, I also send you . . . all authority is given to me, going therefore teach ye all nations . . . whose soever sins you remit, they are remitted unto them, and whose soever sins you retain, they are retained"; and to St Peter above all he gives the privilege of immovable faith, and the power to bind and to loose. You see, then, that our Lord from the first meant his Church to centre round a hierarchy; took more trouble, you may say, about forming the character and confirming the faith of the Church's future rulers than about baptizing people or making converts; indeed, when he ascended into heaven, the Church he left behind him was only a Church of 120 souls. But he had the nucleus; he had the *cadre* of his army, the rank and file could wait. And that means, clearly, that it was his intention to leave behind him an institution with a visible membership, with rules, with officials, in a word, an organized Church.

All that is so plain that I am almost ashamed to remind you of it. But I think you will find, the more you go about among Protestants, that this whole idea of our Lord's career has been left out of sight in most of the theologies of to-day. They talk as if he merely meant us to acquire from him a certain outlook upon life, and to mould our characters accordingly; or at any rate to observe certain rules of conduct; or at most to believe certain things which he told us about his heavenly Father, and the forgiveness of sins, and the world to come. God knows he did mean us to do all that, and we do some of it, most of us, very imperfectly. But there is something that comes before all that, is presupposed by all that; before we do anything for his sake, or believe anything on his assurance, he wants us to *be* something; to be members of his Church. He wants to incorporate us into himself by incorporating us into a living society, continuous from his day to ours. We know, of course, that those who are outside the Church and remain outside the Church in good faith can be saved by that title. And we have no idea, we don't profess to have any idea, how many millions of souls that qualification will include. All we do know is that however numerous they are, they are exceptions. The right way to enter eternal life begins—it doesn't end, heaven knows, but it begins—with visible membership of Christ's true Church.

So, if you get arguing with your non-Catholic friends about religion, you mustn't let them think that we Catholics differ from them over one or two additional points of doctrine which we believe and they don't, like indulgences or the infallibility of the Pope. The question over which we differ from them is a fundamental one, which precedes all other discussion and all other possibilities of agreement or disagreement. We believe that the first requisite of the Christian vocation is to belong to a particular religious body, the religious body which is represented in England by the Cardinal Archbishop of Westminster and those other bishops who are in communion with him. If you don't belong to that body, it doesn't make the slightest difference whether you believe in indulgences, or the infallibility of the Pope, or anything of that kind; mere believing won't help you, unless you enjoy, or are prepared to accept, membership of the one visible Church of Christ. And therefore it is of fundamental importance for any soul which is really seeking the truth to discover which that one visible Church of Christ is.

The creed which will be said in your name a few moments from now, the Nicene Creed, as they call it, affirms belief among other things in One Holy Catholic and Apostolic Church. Now, we are not alone in making that claim for ourselves. The Churches of the East, out of Communion with the See of Rome, use the same words at the corresponding point in their liturgy; so does the Church of England, except that for some reason or other the word "Holy" has disappeared from the description. It is said to have been a printer's error; the printer may have had his tongue in his cheek; anyhow, there it stands. But the Anglican claim is evidently meant to be the same. Now, in which of those three bodies—each of them is a visible, organized body of Christians—shall we find this common claim justified? Not until he has decided that question can a man be certain that he has taken the first step, the very first step, in fulfilling the will of our Lord Jesus Christ.

And, as I say, it is the tradition of Catholic apologetics that we establish our claim to be *the* Church which our Lord founded, by showing that the religious body to which we belong exhibits these four notes or marks. That is how we distinguish it from other religious bodies for which the same claim might be made. You see, the old Church or assembly of Jews did not need any marks to distinguish it. To belong to it, with full membership at any rate, you had to be a Jew; and the centre of its worship was naturally Jerusalem, the Jewish capital. But this new Church which our Lord founded had no such qualification of nationality; had not, as yet, any local centre round which its loyalties could rally. Evidently, there was the danger that in course of time you would get two bodies of people, either of which claimed to be the true Church. And, to adjudicate those claims, it was necessary that the true Church should bear certain distinguishing characteristics. Some of them arise from the very nature of the case; some depend on our Lord's own directions, given to his apostles while he was still on earth. Let us run through them very briefly.

The Church has to be one, in the nature of the case, if it is to be a visible Church at all. Our Lord made certain promises, of vast moment, to his followers and to their successors. If there are to be two bodies of people, each claiming with plausible arguments to be the true Church, then one must be right and the other wrong; otherwise we could not be certain that our Lord's promises had descended to both, or to either. If, therefore, schisms happen within the body of Christendom, the result of such schism is not to produce two Churches of Christ; what you have left is one true Church of Christ and one schismatic body; otherwise, after all these centuries, we should no longer be certain that our Lord's promises held good.

He has further laid it down, that his Church should be distinguished by sanctity. Not in the sense that all Christians are holy, however desirable that might be; or even that the rulers of the Church should at all times be recognizably holy people; he will not interfere with the freedom of our wills to that extent. But his true Church will always be *productive* of saints. These signs shall follow them that believe; in my name they shall cast out devils, they shall lay hands on the sick, and they shall recover, and if they drink any deadly thing, it shall not hurt them. Those special graces with which our Lord delights his saints to honour will not be the property of one age, they will appear in all ages, and the true Church will always be able to point to them as an element in her sanctity.

And again, our Lord insists that his Church is to be Catholic; "Going, teach *all* nations." Generally speaking, it will be possible in the event of schism to say, "Here on the one side is a local body of Christians, all belonging to one race or one geographical area, pertinaciously clinging to their own national traditions, and on the other side you have the great body of Christian people." It is to that principle that St Augustine always appeals in his controversy with the Donatists. In Africa, you had two bodies of Christians, out of Communion with one another; yet either held the true faith, either came down from the apostles, either administered valid sacraments. How are you to distinguish which was the right body to belong to? Why, on the very simple principle that one of them was purely African, had no representatives in the rest of the world, whereas the other was in visible communion with the whole of Christendom.

And, lest even that test should be insufficient, as it might be when it seemed that the whole world was being divided into East and West, or that the whole of Europe was being divided into North and South, we must recognize that the Church is to be not only Catholic but Apostolic; must trace its descent by unbroken tradition from the Apostles. It must preserve the continuous tradition of the priesthood, by the laying on of hands; every priest must be able to say, "Such and such a bishop ordained me." And there must be continuity of jurisdiction; "As the Father hath sent me, even so *send* I you"; the care of a given group of human souls was to belong, not to any chance preacher at the street corner who felt moved to get up and testify, but to a pastor duly commissioned by the general body of Christians to undertake that office. And lastly, there must be continuity of faith; if it can be proved that any body of Christians has abandoned the teaching of the first Christians, or has so watered it down that it is no longer recognizable, then that body of Christians, however good and devoted they may be, is something other than the true Church.

Those are the points we shall be considering this term; and though they seem elementary enough, they are of an importance not to be estimated by their place in mere controversy. They have a bearing on our duty as Catholics, and on the witness we ought to bear, as Catholics, in a world which has so largely forgotten the Christian message.

X

THE UNHOLINESS OF THE CHURCH

THE second mark of the Church, her sanctity, demands more careful and fuller treatment from us than the remaining ones. Because in all the other instances it is we who have the obvious case, the *prima facie* case, to support us; it is our adversaries or our rivals who have to explain, and to distinguish, and to qualify, and to hum and haw and beat about the bush generally before they attempt to establish their conclusions, not without the suspicion of special pleading. Thus, when we talk about the unity of the Church, we can appeal to visible facts; to the existence of a world-wide organization which is as much a body corporate with a central management as (to use Dean Inge's uncomplimentary parallel) the Standard Oil Company. Whereas any other form of Christianity has to adopt the old Oxford formula and say, "It depends what you mean by unity"; and so introduce us to the notion of a unity which lies in the past, somewhere in the first six centuries, or in the future, assuming that the future ever comes off. So with Catholicity; our Church evidently embraces under a single formula peoples of widely different nationalities, and habits of thought, and stages of culture. Whereas Protestant Christianity makes very little appeal to certain types of culture, the Latin for example; and even so it is only by a considerable stretch of the imagination that you can think of Protestant Christendom as a uniform system; is Bishop Barnes, for example, really a fellow-believer of those American negroes whose notions of theology are reflected in the play called *Green Pastures*? So with Apostolicity; the continuity of our Church with the Church of the Catacombs and of the Cenacle is a plain fact which you can only deny at your own intellectual peril; you may say that our doctrines have developed, that our notions of Christianity have become distorted, that we have become hard, and exclusive, and standardized as the centuries have rolled over us; but no one in his senses can deny that ever since our Lord spoke the words "As the Father hath sent me, I also send you" there has been a continuous line of mission; so that I can trace my orders to Cardinal Bourne, and he to the Catholic Bishop who ordained him, and so on and so on, if the registers of the Church had been kept exhaustively, right back to the times of the apostles themselves. Whereas it is our Anglican friends who have to take us for long excursions into the history of the sixteenth century, and tell us how Bonner was intruded into the See of London, though it is an odd fact that the person who intruded him was in Anglican theory the supreme Head of the Church in England. All through, you see, it is *they* who have a difficult job to establish their contentions, whereas *we* can merely point to the facts.

But in this matter of sanctity, our case is not by any means so evident. True, so far as the external marks of sanctity are concerned, we can point out that in our Church miracles are a constantly expected occurrence, whereas outside the Church they are claimed but rarely, and at times of special religious revival. Or we can insist that the life of the cloister is natural to the Catholic Church, whereas in the non-Catholic denominations that life is either wholly absent, or is a late and uncertain development. But when you come to look at Protestants as a whole, and Catholics as a whole, our *prima facie* case is by no means so strong. Indeed, many people would tell you that the Protestants have a stronger *prima facie* case than ourselves. As I remember I put it once, it is probably less safe to leave your umbrella at the door of a Catholic church than at the door of a Methodist chapel. Elsewhere, the marks of the Church lie plain on the surface; when it comes to the mark of holiness, we have to dig for it.

And there's another difference, which for the moment I will only indicate briefly. You and I can't make the Church more one than she is; we can't make the Church more Catholic than she is; we can't make the Church more Apostolic than she is. But we can—well, I won't say we can make the Church more holy than she is, but we can make the Church *look* more holy than she does, we can extend the area of her sanctity and develop its possibilities, by the common actions of our ordinary daily lives.

Now, what are the reasons for this impression, common in English-speaking countries, that Protestants are well-behaved, decent sort of people, whereas Catholics, take them all round, are a low lot? Well, there's one explanation which does no discredit to us. The Catholic religion is one of the natural religions of the world, not a religion of the sacristy or a religion of the Sunday school tea-fight; and Catholic piety, in consequence, can flourish in surroundings which are still, by the Puritan judgments of the English mind, accounted risky or even disreputable. And there's no doubt, I suppose, that if you went through a list of what I may call the morally dangerous trades, of all the walks of life which one's aunts didn't approve of, actors and actresses and bookmakers and jockeys and prizefighters and the rest of it, you would find a very high proportion of professing Catholics as compared with professing Protestants; much higher than if you went through the grocers and the haberdashers and the undertakers and so on. It may be partly a question of nationality, but I think it is largely a question of opportunity. While Puritanism was strong, Catholics went into the professions which Protestants didn't like to go into because they were not quite nice; and, by force of tradition, even now when Puritanism has grown weaker, Catholics go into those professions still.

To that extent, the impression that we Catholics are an unholy set of people is ill-founded. But I'm afraid it's perfectly true, and more true than most people realize, that a good many of the world's rogues are Catholics. It's extraordinary how often you will come across Catholic names when you are reading in the newspaper the records of crime, whether on a small scale or on a large scale. I expect you know the story of the Catholic chaplain at Sing-Sing, who was explaining to a visitor how unscrupulously and uncharitably people talked about the Church. "Why," he is reported to have said, "you will actually hear people say that all the prisoners who are executed at Sing-Sing are Catholics. Whereas I can assure you that there are five prisoners now awaiting execution, and one of them's a Jew." Now, it's perfectly true that in a way this unholiness of Catholics is a compliment to our religion. Because it does mean that a Catholic does not necessarily cease to be a Catholic because he is a rogue. He knows what is right even when he is doing what is wrong. The Protestant as a rule will give up his faith first and his morals afterwards; with Catholics it is the other way round. The Protestant only feels his religion to be true as long as he goes on practising it; the Catholic feels the truth of his religion as something independent of himself, which does not cease to be valid when he, personally, fails to live up to its precepts. But I think there's more to it than that. I think it's quite probably true that when a Catholic does go wrong he—or she—goes worse than other people.

After all, theologically speaking, there is nothing whatever to be surprised at in that. When you think of all the means of grace a Catholic has had; the clearness of the teaching he has

4

received, the positiveness of his conviction; the sacrament of penance to give him frequent opportunities of amendment, to bestow grace by which that amendment might have been achieved; his Communions, the privilege of becoming one with Christ, made Deiform, when he approached the altar; the example of holy lives lived around him, the influence, very often, of a devout Catholic home—if a man starts with all those spiritual privileges and yet makes a mess of his life, is it wonderful as a matter of psychology that he should react to the other extreme; is it wonderful as a matter of theology that the grace which has wooed him so patiently should weary of its patience at last? I do not mean, of course, that grace altogether deserts him; there is hope for the most abandoned, and God knows there may be plenty of souls now in prisons and penitentiaries that will find their way to heaven sooner than you and I. But that the holiest Church should produce the greatest sinners is but the natural application of the principle that the corruption of the best is the worst.

The ordinary Protestant, then, is vaguely aware that certain Catholics live remarkably holy lives, shut up in convents or in monasteries. He sees young men from Campion Hall going out to lectures, looking good, and he thinks it rather a fine thing that there should be men living such beautifully disciplined lives, though he is quite certain that it would not do for him. On the other hand, he has only got to read up the murder trials and such other parts of the news in the Sunday papers as are more attentively followed, to find out that there are people bearing Catholic names, brought up in Catholic schools, who do no credit to the system at all. If, therefore, he is in search of a religion, and if (like most Englishmen) he is prepared to judge of a religion mainly by the type of character it produces, he is driven back, in fairness, to contemplating the lives of Catholics who are neither particularly saints nor particularly sinners, people like you and me. And that, as I say, is where this second mark of the Church comes home to us personally.

I know what you are going to say. You are going to say that it is a poor motive for living a virtuous life, to live it for the sake of its effect on other people; to be always looking out of the corner of your eye to see whether there's a proctor watching you not going into the *George* bar. Well, of course, I mean nothing of the sort. I don't mean that there is any motive for living a virtuous life which is either worth having or worth admiring except the love of God and the desire to imitate Jesus Christ. But it is true that in countries like our own, and in a society like that of Oxford, where Catholics mingle freely with other people and come under the close scrutiny of other people, the Catholic who lives carelessly commits, in however slight a degree, an added sin of scandal. It is necessary, our Lord says, that scandals should come, but woe to that man through whom they come. If all Catholics were saints, the truth of our religion would become too glaringly obvious, and there would be no real exercise of faith in making one's submission to the Church. That Catholics, from the Pope downwards, should sometimes give scandal to people outside the Church, is according to the consequent will of God. But woe to the man through whom the scandal comes; through him, that mark of holiness which should be one of the Church's most distinguishing characteristics has failed to shine out, for one questioning mind, for one tortured conscience. "Nor knowest thou what argument thy life to thy neighbour's creed hath lent"—don't imagine that because comparatively few men up here are received into the Church, that is the measure of our responsibilities. One is always hearing of people who were up here perhaps five or six years ago becoming Catholics. And in the story of their search for the truth, what they had seen of Catholic life in Oxford counted for something. It was a *pro* or a *con*; and your life, in all probability, will be a *pro* or a *con* for some-body, somebody you've lost touch with, lost sight of, but who will come to ask himself later, "Does that theory square with what one sees in real life? Is it supported, or is it contra-dicted, by the behaviour of the Catholics I have known?" And that will mean you.

Well, I've left myself very little time, and I hope you have very little need, for an application of the moral. But, though most of you are tired by now of hearing me say what you are going to hear me say, I hope you will bear with me when I say it; it is a familiar theme. Do try to believe me when I tell you that you Catholics are, in your generation, the city set on a hill, the salt designed to be the salt of the earth, of which our Lord spoke in his sermon on the Mount. I say, in your genera-tion; it was not true to the same extent in my own. Of course, Catholics ought always to be the salt of the earth, but the earth has never wanted salting so badly as now. Catholics ought always to be the city set on a hill, but I suppose there has never been a time since the Reformation, at which Catho-lics were set so prominently on a hill as they are just now. I say, do try to believe me; you will think that I am talking grey-beard's cant, preacher's commonplaces, but it is not that. There is a time of life at which you are like a man on the crest of a hill, who can see the traffic climbing up one side and going down the other, both at once; that is when you are in middle age, and have lost the self-preoccupation of youth without reaching the fixity of view which comes with elderly life. And I am absolutely certain that in this new generation of English people, your generation, it is the Catholic body which has got to save our civilization, because nothing else will. All the other things we lived by are going under. The salt of the earth? and if the salt lose its savour, wherewith shall it be salted? Have salt in yourselves, our Lord says; it is you that must have the reserves of energy, the positive influence which radiates; you are not to take your standards from other people; it is the other people who are to take their standards from you.

And, of course, it's hard for you to see that. You come up, very largely, from schools where the Catholic tradition was in force, where the natural thing to do was the right thing to do. You find here a crowd of people of your own age, superficially of the same culture as yourselves, and it seems natural to go on doing what you have been accustomed to do, swimming with the stream, taking your colour from people round you. You feel rather small, coming into such a world of new experience, and very naturally; lots of your friends seem so much cleverer, so much more experienced in the ways of life than you. And it is the easiest thing in the world for you to pick up, without noticing it, something of their hopelessly vague attitude about religion and the world, about right and wrong, about what matters and whether anything matters. You don't fall in, please God, with the loose views many of them have about elementary morals, about sex and purity in particular; but you begin to think of the moral ideals which you have been taught as if they were an ecclesiastical code, belonging only to us Catholics, and binding only on us Catholics, instead of being what they are—God's law, his law for everybody. You fall into slack ways, and worldly ways, and riotous ways, out of mere human respect, because people up here seem to do that sort of thing; weak fools, throwing away with both hands your Catholic birthright.

But the Master whom we follow was holy, separated from sinners; and he has made his Church holy; and his will is to find that holiness visibly reflected, for all the world to see, in you.

XI

WHEAT IN THE COCKLE

HE parable of the wheat and the cockle is really one of a pair; people often don't realize that, because the sister parable does not follow straight on it, but at an interval of several verses, though they are both in the same chapter. The sister parable, as I call it, is the one in which our Lord compares the kingdom of heaven to a net which is let down into the sea and draws up a great quantity of fish, both bad and good. Either parable is an answer to the question, "Do all Christians go to heaven?" And the answer is "No." And if you ask why, either parable supplies the same explanation; God does not want it to be known, in this life, which souls are his and which will meet with final rejection; it is better for our faith that we should belong to a Church which has imperfect as well as perfect members; better for our watchfulness over ourselves that we should realize the possibility of being a baptized Christian, and yet not bound for heaven.

Let me draw that out a little. The field in which the wheat and the cockle are sown is the world; our Lord has told us that; but the crop of grain, bad and good alike, is, I think, the Church. It is in the Church, not simply in the world, that bad and good grow together side by side. And the servants of the householder, that is, the angels, are represented as saying, "Shall we root up the cockle; shall we exterminate the wicked, as they were exterminated at the time of the Deluge, and leave only the righteous to live?" And they are told, "No, wait till the harvest, that is, till the judgment, and then the distinction will be made clear; *then* shall the just shine forth in the kingdom of their Father." So in the other parable, good fish and worthless fish alike must be carried in the net; it is only when the boat reaches the shore that they will be separated, and the worthless fish will be thrown away; *then* shall the just shine forth in the kingdom of their Father. Till then, you will have people who wear the sign of Christ on their foreheads and take his name upon their lips, who will not be able to resign their souls into his hands, with full contrition, at the last terrible moment of their lives.

If we are asked, "How can we be certain that God has revealed himself to mankind?" that question can't be answered all in one mouthful. We need a convergent proof to make sure that there is one true revelation, and that the Christian revelation is that one. And one piece of evidence we want to adduce is the mere fact of Christendom, what it has meant in history, what it means to-day, the way in which it meets the needs and solves the difficulties of common living. Logically, of course, such a proof couldn't stand by itself for a moment; but taken with the others it has weight. Only, when we have admitted all that, isn't there, we are tempted to ask, another side to it all? Mustn't we remember at the same time the shortcomings of Christendom as we know it, and balance these against the considerations we adduced in its favour? And indeed, it's not difficult to imagine the line of argument which would be adopted by our opponents in this matter; let us sketch it to ourselves for a moment.

"You claim," says our adversary, "that your Church, alone among the institutions of the world, has defied the centuries; but consider how much stronger it once was, at least in external influence, than it is now; are we certain that it is not a machine which is running down? You claim that it is world-wide; so it is, but think of the vast tracts of the world in which its adherents are few and scattered; think how many people die every day who have scarcely even heard of Christianity. You tell us that it has been a great civilizing influence; but how many reforms, such as the abolition of slavery, had to wait for long centuries, Christian centuries, before they were effected; think how many cruelties have been practised before now, how many frauds, how many acts of oppression, in the name of the Church. You say that it has preached a consistent moral message, but look at the long record of worldliness in high places, of Popes, even, who set the moral law openly at defiance. You tell us that Christendom has been the mother of the arts; but think of the revolting ugliness you find in so many modern Catholic churches; think of the church repositories. You tell us that Christianity meets all the needs of mankind; but if so, why have we seen, in our own time, so many plausible substitutes for it which have captured the imagination of many among our contemporaries; Christian Science, which tells you that you do not know how to deal with the problem of suffering; Spiritualism, which tells you that you are not courageous enough in your attitude towards death?

"Might it not have been expected," they argue, "that if this Christian revelation of yours was really meant to be the final revelation of God to man, its credentials would have been presented to us in a still more impressive form, so that all logical doubt of its divine origin would have been excluded? Might we not have expected that all Christian bishops would have been holy men, that all religious orders would have retained their pristine exactness of observance, instead of falling into relaxation and needing reform? Might we not have expected that Christianity would still inspire the arts, and initiate movements of philanthropy, instead of eyeing both with suspicion, and sometimes meeting them with hostility? Might we not have expected that all Christians in our own day would be distinguishable by that gracious mark which singled them out in the old pagan world, when men said, '*See how these Christians love one another*'? In a word, if God meant the existence of Christendom to be, if not the proof of his revelation, at least its most signal advertisement, would he not have been at pains to make it a little easier for us? To make it impossible for anybody to come in contact with it and not immediately hail it as the truth, unless sheer prejudice held him back from the confession?"

All that can be said; all that is said, and is perhaps in most men's minds—for we live in days when people are not fond of speculative thought, preferring concrete issues—the most powerful motive at work in hindering the advance of Christianity. But the answer to it doesn't take much finding, and it is this; that if the Christian religion had borne upon its face such unmistakable marks of a significance more than human, we should be forced, as it were, into accepting its claims; there would be no room for doubt in the matter, and consequently no room for faith; we should accept the Christian revelation as unthinkingly as we accept the common facts of our exterior life, without any process of mental discipline, any spirit of adventure in our choice. Imagine what it would be like if, as soon as the first persecutions were over, the Church had immediately stood out in undimmed majesty, with no schisms, no heresies, no exasperating friction with the secular powers to chequer her history; if every Pope had become impeccable at the moment when he became infallible, and Alexander the Sixth had turned into a Savonarola at the instant when the triple tiara was put on his head; if all the triumphs of the Church had been achieved bloodlessly, and all had been utilized immediately for the evident good of mankind; if there had never been such a thing as a worldly

4*

bishop, or an idle monk, or a venal friar; if there had been no Reformation to rend the body of Christendom, if there were no rival religions to dispute with Catholicism the allegiance of the human heart—wouldn't it all be too obvious, too plain sailing? Our Lord, it is quite evident, didn't contemplate anything of that kind. It is necessary to the world, he said, *necessary*, that scandals should come; it is part of our probation, he would have us understand, that we should be puzzled by all these anomalies of religious history, and distressed at them, and yet have enough strength of resolution to see behind them and beyond them, and recognize the Church as his own Bride, the inheritor of his promises and the completion of his life.

Well, then, we are not going to treat the Christian revelation as something self-evidently true, something that bears the stamp of its own genuineness printed large on every page of its history. The fact of Christendom is not a *proof* to the world that God spoke through Christ; it is rather a challenge to the world to consider whether God did not speak through Christ. It is possible for us to doubt it, just as it is possible to doubt the existence of God himself. He has given us sufficient proofs of his existence, and some knowledge, even, of his own Nature, from the use of our unaided human reason. But we must *use* it; we must apply our minds to the problem, search for the truth, not expect it to fall straight into our mouths for the asking. You can doubt God's existence by simply not bothering about it; and he does not interfere, commonly, by any sensational advertisement of his power such as would force our minds back to him—he does not strike every perjurer dead, or every blasphemer dumb. That would be to force us into belief; and that is not his way. So here, in this matter of the credentials with which his revelation comes to us. There are credentials, but we have got to look for them. We have got to cast our minds back across the gulf of history, to days very remote from our own; we have got to concentrate our attention upon one corner of the world, not, even in those days, a very important corner of the world; we have got to put ourselves in the position of men very different from ourselves in race, in culture, and in outlook. We have got to go back to the life of Jesus of Nazareth, isolating the life-centre from which this vast organism of Christianity has sprung.

And when we do that, when we go right back to the origins of our religion, we shall see at once which elements in the history of Christendom are native to it and fully representative of its genius, which are accidental and false developments. In the parable, you see, the wheat was sown first; the cockle appeared only through a hostile afterthought; if we go back to the life of Christ, we shall find what seed he sowed, and which is the legitimate crop that has sprung from his teaching. Thus, we shall claim that the Christian revelation is true, because our Lord fulfilled, in the whole manner of his appearance and in the whole scheme of his life, the prophecies made to the Jews long before about the Messiah who was to come and deliver them. Whether you look at isolated texts in the Old Testament, or at the broad outline of the Messianic hope, you will find, in the Gospels, its exact and yet unexpected fulfilment. The events of our Lord's Life are the key which fits the lock of Old Testament prophecy. What wonder then if we find that the Church which he founded, his own mystical Body and the visible continuation of his Incarnate Life, meets the expectations and answers the needs of every age in history; interprets mankind to itself, inspires its art and fosters its genius—now more, now less, but always with a kind of natural appropriateness? What wonder if in every age and in every part of the world souls, very different in their stage of development and in the range of their capacities, find in the practice of the Christian religion the fulfilment of their highest instincts? "Art thou he that should come, or do we look for another?" The question answers itself; nobody looks for another revelation, even in these late days; the world accepts his revelation, or resigns itself to its despairs.

Again, we shall claim that the Christian revelation is true because his miracles, culminating in the unique miracle of his Resurrection, can neither be disregarded on historical grounds, nor yet be philosophically explained, unless they were meant to set the seal upon an authentic mission from God to man. The lame walk, the deaf hear, the lepers are cleansed, the dead are raised up—so our Lord himself appeals to his wonderful works to bear testimony of him. What manner of man is this, his followers asked themselves, that the wind and the sea obey him? What wonder, then, if we find his Church in history capable of the most extraordinary conquests, meeting and vanquishing paganism in no strength but that of her own inherent vitality, assimilating and taming the barbarian elements that flooded into Europe in the Dark Ages, holding her own against the stubborn nationalisms of mediæval Europe? What wonder if she, who lives with the life of her Risen Master, dies so many deaths and achieves so many resurrections; survives the Mahomedan attack, survives the Reformation, survives the French Revolution, seems to gain strength, even in our own day, from all the efforts that are made to disintegrate the civilization which she gave us? "I have power to lay down my life, and power to take it again." Wherever faith in the miracle of the Resurrection strikes deep root, the miracle of the Resurrection repeats itself.

And we shall claim that the Christian revelation is true because the character and the teaching of our Blessed Lord, though it is only preserved for us in a few fragmentary records, has the power to arrest human admiration and to claim human sympathy as no other living force yet had. The proof for the existence of God was a convergent proof. So it is with the proof we are discussing at present; our belief in the authenticity of the Christian revelation is based on man's expectation of Christ, on the evidence of Christ's power, and on the evidence of his goodness. We would not claim belief for a Christ who enjoyed miraculous powers, but offered no moral inspiration, nor yet for a Christ who claimed our moral sympathy, but showed no powers which exceeded those of our common nature. So we base our argument partly on his miracles, but partly on his character, on the atmosphere which surrounded him, that fragrance which breathed from him, so that men came away from listening to his simple direct methods of preaching with the feeling, "never man spoke like this Man." What wonder, then, if his saints in every age have caught and handed on in their measure, the kindling enthusiasm of his appeal? The saints, after all, are the best advertisement the Christian religion ever had. And we know that the saints are really the characteristic products of Christendom, its natural fruit, when we have looked back at the life of Jesus of Nazareth, to find all their inspiration centred, and all their light focused, in his.

XII

FAITH LOST AND FOUND

THE general notion of living by faith is not peculiar to Catholics, or to Christians, or even to religiously minded people. Everybody who is not content merely to live for the day and get the most enjoyment he can out of pottering round the world aimlessly, wants, and demands, a faith of some sort to live by. He wants it, because it is man's nature to repose his confidence in something outside himself, something other than himself; only a prig or a fool really sets out with the idea of being self-reliant. Man is happy in the long run only when he is giving himself, and so far as he succeeds in giving himself, to something other than himself; only when he is working for a cause or a creed or a personality to which he can devote himself, with some kind of assurance that he is not wasting his time in doing so. And that kind of assurance can only be achieved by faith—if we take faith in its widest, its most human, its least supernatural acceptation.

What then do we mean by faith in this broad sense? Tennyson, in a well-known passage, referred to it as "believing where we cannot prove." I think he was wrong; proof is a vague word, and I do not see that it is in the least difficult to adhere by faith, whether human or divine faith, to a proposition which to you, at any rate, seems proved. And indeed, I should very strongly object to the imputation that the Catholic Faith cannot be proved; it can. The proof is largely, almost entirely, an *a priori* one, but it is proof nevertheless. And it is quite possible to have human faith in some political doctrine, say, for example, the doctrine of free trade, although you believe that its principles can be demonstrated by economic arguments, and are prepared to adduce such arguments to anybody who will be patient enough to listen to them. I would suggest that a far better definition would be "believing where we cannot *test*." It is impossible for an educated person to believe by faith in the statement that the square on the hypotenuse of a right-angled triangle is equal to the sum of the squares on the other two sides. It is impossible because, assuming the validity of Euclidean space and not worrying with Einstein, the thing can be made evident by demonstration, without leaving even the abstract possibility that the assertion may be wrong; it is not merely that the thing can be proved; it can be proved to the satisfaction of anyone who is capable of following a geometrical argument. Faith only begins when the proposition to which you assent is one that is doubted, or might quite conceivably be doubted, by people of equal intelligence with yourself.

And I say boldly that all men who have ideals—and the people who have no ideals in this world are always dull and generally unhappy—live by some kind of faith, by committing themselves to some kind of loyalty which is not universally recognized as the common property of all thinking men. They must have something, something outside themselves, to make them feel that life is worth living, that good rather than evil is the explanation of the world, that conduct does matter and that right and wrong do exist, if they are going to go on living at all. It is not a theology they demand, particularly, it is just something outside themselves to keep them going, to keep their heads above water, to save themselves from the alternative of committing suicide or collecting postage stamps. And, as I say, you will find that there are three things which can exercise such influence on a man's life; a personality, a philosophy, or a Cause to which he can devote himself.

The influence of a personality may take the form of a great love. Probably it does take that form more often than we think; we are all inclined to be a little cynical and disrespectful in our attitude to other people's love affairs. There are really people who find life worth living because they are allowed, often with very little in the way of recognition or return, to serve and to reverence a woman they love. Or it may be hero-worship for somebody whose intellect, whose character, whose prominence fascinates you. All this demands faith; for your estimate of the personality which means so much to you is not a thing which can be tested or proved by any form of demonstration; you believe in the person who so dominates your life, and it is the very fact that your belief in him has an element of uncertainty in it that makes the whole thing worth while. A person might play you false, might prove unworthy of your admiration; it is precisely that "might" which makes the thing worth while. It is because you are uncertain that it is possible for you to have faith; and with that faith happiness comes into your life, and you find a new attitude towards the world.

Or again the faith on which a man relies, the star to which he hitches his waggon, may be a philosophy, a system of beliefs. Ordinarily he will describe this as a religion, especially in England, where almost anything will pass for a religion. Even the people who believe that the earth is flat regard themselves, I understand, as a religious sect. (By the way, those people are a very good example of how it is possible to have faith in a thing which, for you, is a matter of proof, though one which cannot actually be tested. They think they can prove that the earth is flat, and they will talk to you by the hour about it; and yet, because they find so many people difficult to convince on the point, they adhere to their beliefs with positive fanaticism.) But it is not necessary that the philosophy which makes a man's life worth living for him should be a religious philosophy. And the strangest proof of that is that a small handful of people who really think they can prove that there is no God are prepared to preach that doctrine and write books about it and edit newspapers about it, for all the world as if it was a religion. And those people, so oddly constituted is the human mind, do really derive from their absence of religion something of the satisfaction of feeling they are crusaders.

Or the faith by which a man lives may be faith in a cause or a movement, an institution of some kind whose influence he devotes himself to spreading and popularizing. A political party, or a nationalist movement, or a temperance agitation, or even something quite dull and uninspiring like freemasonry may be the mainspring of his life; it does not matter, you see, so long as there is something outside himself to which he can devote himself, a thing whose advantages are not so obvious to the world in general as they are to himself.

Now, those of us who are baptized and brought up as Catholics are in this position of advantage, that instead of having to look about the world and find for ourselves some loyalty which will make life worth living for us, we are provided, from our cradle upwards, with such a loyalty all ready made. It does not in the least prevent us from adopting other loyalties if we will, from attaching ourselves to any reputable movement or adhering to any sensible philosophy. But it makes that unnecessary; so long as we retain the Catholic faith we have always one interest, one loyalty, one enthusiasm in the world to keep us alive. And the faith, you see, is something much bigger than a mere philosophy. It does commit us to a philosophy; but it does also take us out of ourselves by throwing our reliance on a Personality, the Personality of Jesus Christ; it does also take us out of ourselves by identifying us with a movement, whose triumphs are our triumphs, whose anxieties are our anxieties; life can never be dull for us while the Church is still militant, still has a battle to fight and a position to be vindicated.

I say the faith is something much bigger than a mere philosophy; it involves us in a special attitude towards this world and the world to come. It engages not our minds merely but our whole selves. Yet it depends and must depend from first to last upon an intellectual conviction. It is true that there are certain Nonconformist sects which practically invite you to rely on the Personality of our Lord without ever stopping to consider whether he was Incarnate God or not. It is true that there are politicians, the *Action Française* group, for example, who invite you to admire the Church and to fight for its ascendancy without caring in the least whether the Christian religion is true. But those are aberrations of human sentiment; as a matter of common sense no thinking man will make Christ the centre of his life unless he is intellectually convinced that Christ was God, or will make the Church the focus of his loyalties unless he is intellectually convinced that the Church's origins are divine.

Faith, then, in its central essence, presupposes a judgment of the intellect, a judgment first that God exists; next that he has revealed himself in Jesus Christ, and finally that the Catholic Church is the accredited vehicle of Christ's revelation, and that what she teaches comes to us, consequently, with that certainty which belongs to the Voice of God. But is faith *merely* an intellectual calculation? It cannot, obviously, be that; faith is a virtue, and there can be no virtue in making a mathematical computation; faith is a quality that is more vivid in some Christians than in others, and there could be no such difference of degree if nothing more were demanded of us Christians than a bare intellectual assent. And accordingly the Church, though she will not say with the early Protestants that faith is a quality which is centred in the will, teaches that this quality, centred as it is in the intellect, is nevertheless under the direction of the will. Now, how is that possible? If the Catholic religion is reasonable, how can faith come into it at all? And if it is unreasonable, how can we possibly be justified in making an act of the will which enables us to believe in it?

The answer to that may sound illogical, but nothing is more certain as a matter of experience than this—that where we are asked to form a judgment which is based on any kind of hearsay evidence, we shall not have the energy, or if you will, the courage, to form such a judgment unless we are prepared to make an effort of the will. However fully you read the report of a trial, or the sources for some period of history, you may still be tempted, through prejudice, to withhold your assent from the conclusions, although you can find no flaw in the process; to overcome that prejudice will need an act of the will. And even where no positive prejudice is at work, there is a prejudice which lurks deep in our natures at all times, partly from a kind of indolence and partly from a kind of cowardice—a prejudice, I mean, against affirming anything, against identifying ourselves with a positive judgment, when it is so much simpler to take refuge in humming and hawing and saying, "Yes, I suppose so." There is all the difference in the world, practically, between saying, "Yes, I suppose that is true," and saying, "By Gad, that's true!" And the difference between the two attitudes arises, really, not out of the strength of the evidence before us, but out of our willingness to identify ourselves with the judgment which our reason ratifies. It ought not to be so; it would not be so if we were mere thinking machines; but we are not mere thinking machines, and for that reason it takes an act of the will, however slight, before we can affirm something which, although it is not self-evident, we can nevertheless see to be true.

Faith comes in to encourage us, when we are hesitating to make an affirmation; and that is why we can say that faith is a gift—there is a bestowal of grace which confirms our wills, and makes it possible for us to assert, and to go on asserting, truths of religion over which, if we were left to our indolent and cowardly selves, we might be tempted to suspend judgment. That is why faith can be exercised in equal measure, and is needed in equal measure, by a trained theologian and by a simple peasant. If faith were a mere affair of the intellect, then the theologian would need a greater measure of faith, or at least a different kind of faith, as compared with the peasant. But it is not so; either needs the same gift, either has the same moral responsibility—that of asserting positively what he sees to be true, and identifying himself whole-heartedly with the assertion. The theologian understands the doctrine with all its niceties and interpretations, as far as it is possible for the human mind to understand such things; the peasant understands it in terms of his own thought, using crude analogies and words inadequate to the situation. But either needs, and either might lose, the gift of faith which transforms, for him, a mere intellectual conclusion into a conviction which is really part of himself.

Now, there are two ways in which the faith can be lost. One is by altering your intellectual conclusions until they are no longer in harmony with Christian doctrine, without paying attention to what you are doing. That means that you lose the faith piecemeal; you slip into habits of thought which are inconsistent with Christian theology, although you go on professing to be a Christian all the time; pride, or carelessness, prevents you from seeing where it is that your own thought is leading you. That is what happened, I suppose, to George

Tyrrell; anybody could have told him that the modernist conclusions he was reaching were unsound theology, and would be condemned as soon as anybody took the trouble to condemn them. But he went on, and when the condemnation of his views came, he realized that he had drifted gradually away until his whole mind was utterly out of sympathy with Catholic teaching. That happens, chiefly, to professional theologians, and especially to those whose business it is to explain Catholic theology to people outside the Church. But there is a danger of its happening to ordinary people, and for that reason I do implore you, as Catholics who are living to some extent in an atmosphere of thought, and uncommonly unorthodox thought, to take an intellectual interest in your religion; to know what it teaches, and why it teaches what it does and what answer it makes to the sceptical objections which are launched against its doctrines from outside.

But there is another way of losing your faith, which I suppose is much commoner, and it is this. You do not find difficulties about this or that doctrine, quarrel with this or that affirmation made by the Catholic Church. No, you seem to lose all at once that faculty of affirming truth, of making its assertions your own, which we have seen to be involved in the nature of faith. It is not exactly that the motives for believing in God's existence, or our Lord's Divinity, or the Church's infallibility, look any different to you now as compared with the way they looked yesterday; no, the whole thing looks probable enough, if you force yourself to face the issue, but it does not grip you, does not mean anything to you —your will has altered, not your intellect. You still hold the truth in your hand, but you no longer grasp it.

People suggest that you should read books; you reply that apologetic writings in favour of the Church may, perhaps, appeal to you merely as intellectual statements, but they do not restore to you the power you have lost—the power of affirming the truth of these supernatural facts which come to you on the authority of the Church. What is to be done then? I will venture to face that point, in case there should be any-one here who finds himself in that despairing position, or is in fear that he may fall into it should his present tendencies of of thought go on undisturbed.

It is a rude thing to say, because it is always a rude thing to remind people of their age; but a certain obscuration of the faith is common in your circumstances and at your time of life. There are a multitude of causes which we have no time to discuss, physical, mental, local; but it is a fact of common knowledge that faith becomes less vivid, for most people, at a time of life when they have no longer the boy's capacity for swallowing anything he is told without thinking about it, and have not yet reached the age when the urgency of living and the experience of human insufficiency drives them back on the thought of God. Nobody has put it better than Mr Belloc, in a passage which most of you probably know: "Belief," he says, "of its nature breeds a reaction and an indifference. Those who believe nothing, but only think and judge, cannot understand this. Of its nature it struggles with us. And we, when our youth is full on us, invariably reject it and set out in the sunlight content with natural things. Then for a long time we are like men who follow the downward cleft of a mountain, and the peaks are hidden from us and forgotten. It takes years to reach the dry plain, and then we look back and see our home. What is it, do you think, that causes the return? I think it is the problem of living; for every day, every experience of evil, demands a solution. That solution is provided by the memory of the great scheme which at last we remember. Our childhood pierces through again."

And therefore—if you will pardon me for making such an irreverent attack on your self-confidence—do not be too ready to believe, just because you find your interest in religion waning, that this is loss of faith, or even the beginnings of a loss of faith. It is not really your faith that is tending to disappear; it is merely your boyhood's faculty for taking things for granted, and that is a very different thing from faith. Do not be tempted, for example, to give up attending Mass, with the reflection that it would be hypocrisy for you to go in your present state of mind. That is to assume that your mind has already reached its final position; believe me, you have a long way to travel, for better or for worse, before your thought will become fixed in the groove of a lifetime. And, in the same way, do not give up the practice of saying your prayers. It may be that heaven seems more distant to you than it did; all is not with you as it was yesterday and the day before; but that obscuration of belief will be only temporary, if you will be true to God, and hold on to your faith in the dark.

Here is another suggestion, which may not be without its value—if you find yourself thus apparently deserted by the light of faith, do not fluster and baffle your imagination by presenting to it all the most difficult doctrines of the Christian religion, those which unbelievers find it easiest to attack; do not be for ever asking yourself, "Can I really believe that marriage is indissoluble? Can I really believe that it is possible to go to hell as the punishment of one mortal sin?" Keep your attention fixed on the main point, which is a single point—Can I trust the Catholic Church as the final repository of revealed truth? If you can, all the rest follows, if you cannot, it makes little difference what else you believe, or disbelieve.

XIII

THE UNCONSCIOUS CATHOLIC

EVERY Sunday, more or less, you are told how fortunate you are to be Catholics. And it is almost impossible for us, in listening to such expositions, not to be held up occasionally by a distracting thought: "That's all very well, and it seems full of consolations for *us*; but after all, what about the other people? Most of us here are going about all day with people who aren't Catholics and aren't, as far as we can see, even on the way to becoming Catholics. They are nice people, good-living people many of them; nearly all, if you come to look beneath the surface, have excellent qualities tucked away; where exactly do they get off? Is there no chance for them in eternity? And if there is, how much of a chance is it, and how does it come to them? If we are going to accept the doctrine as apparently we must accept it, *Extra ecclesiam nulla salus*, isn't it going to make us feel rather unhappy about our non-Catholic friends?" So I thought I would devote this morning to a consideration of that question. It is all familiar ground, I hope, to most of you; and it is pretty dull going. But it is important, I think, to have an answer to such difficulties as these, ready for those occasions when our Protestant friends say, "Of course, *you* think I'm going to hell; you have to." Let's just make certain that we don't lay ourselves open to the charge of stuffiness on the one side, or land ourselves in theological misstatements on the other.

The gateway of all sacramental grace, as we know, is baptism. First of all, then, what is the position of the un-baptized? After all, for innumerable centuries before Christ the human race had to get on without the sacrament of bap-tism, and even now there are plenty of people in the world who have never had the chance of being baptized. If it comes to that, there are probably a good many of our friends who have never been baptized; the Jews and the Quakers for example, and the people whose parents didn't hold with going to church at all. Well, when you are considering people like that, it is very important to keep two principles in mind. One is, that baptism is not necessarily baptism by water; there is such a thing as baptism of desire. It is quite certain, I mean, that a person who at the time of his death was anxious to be baptized, but could find nobody to do it for him or no water to do it with, would nevertheless become a member of Christ's Mystical Body through his desire of bap-tism. And we can't, evidently, be certain how far that prin-ciple may not extend; it's certain that the Holy Patriarchs who died in the hope of a Messiah were saved through that hope, and it isn't for us to say how many of the heathen may have been saved through some distant inkling of the same truth; may not be saved in that way even now, provided that the chance of embracing the Christian religion has never effectively come in their way.

And that's where the other principle comes in; it's quite certain that nobody ever has gone to hell or ever will go to hell except through his own fault. It's not the legacy of original sin, it's one's own actual sins, that bring the sentence of eternal reprobation. And if it's true that all men sin, it is equally true that contrition is open to all men as a remedy for sin. There-fore we've no right to assume that anybody has been eternally lost because there is no record in his life that he ever had or desired baptism. I should certainly be very much surprised if

I found myself in a heaven which didn't contain Socrates and Plato and Virgil and plenty of other people who, at first sight, would have no right to be there. How it is that such souls come to be saved we don't know. Some have thought that at the very moment of death, and perhaps even after the moment at which a doctor would give a certificate of medical death, an illumination is given to them which, if they accept it, will achieve the baptism of desire. Others prefer to think that the desire of baptism can be implicitly contained in an act of love towards God, even an act that is confused, even an act that is inarticulate. We don't know; all we do know is, that it is theologically indefensible to say of any man, Nero, for example, or Mahomet, "That man went to hell"; we've no right, even in the extreme case, to despair of God's infinite mercies.

All that, as you see, is only a kind of Christian agnosticism. But when we come on to the case of people who have been baptized but don't ever become Catholics, our ground is much more certain. Every child that is baptized becomes, *ipso facto*, not only a Christian but a Catholic. A child that dies unbaptized, having done nothing to deserve eternal punishment, will enjoy, according to the more common opinion, a state of natural happiness in eternity which falls short, indeed, of the supernatural happiness reserved for Christ's elect, but is nevertheless adequate to its human aspirations. A child which dies after baptism cannot be supposed to achieve the brightness of glory which belongs to those who have striven, and merited, and obtained. But it belongs to the Mystical Body of Christ, and wins its heaven.

Now, supposing that the child lives, how long does it go on being a Catholic? Until it reaches the age of reason; it is quite certain that there are no Protestants in the world under the age of five. You cease to be a Catholic only when, with the full use of your reason, you consent, at least externally, to embrace the beliefs of some other religion; or when you begin to hold, with the full use of your reason, philosophical beliefs opposed to the doctrines of the Church. If you could imagine a child that was baptized and then grew up without giving a single thought to religion for better or worse—that child has become, in strict theory, a very slack Catholic; not a Protestant. And in strict theory, if such a person wanted to join this congregation at the age of nineteen, say, he ought to be given conditional baptism in case his baptism in childhood was for some reason invalid; but he oughtn't to be *received* into the Church with the official form for the reception of converts. Because that form is essentially a renunciation of errors; and the person in question, *ex hypothesi*, has never held any.

What normally happens, of course, is that the child grows up to be seven or eight, and then he is packed off to Sunday school and starts learning to be a Protestant. Whether you say that he does so willingly is, of course, a matter of definition; probably he kicks a good deal at first, especially if it means putting on a clean collar. But the fact remains that he goes; in doing so, does he commit a sin of schism? Materially he does, formally he does not. Let us get those two terms right, because the common instinct of English speech is to use them the wrong way round. If you eat, on a Friday, out of a jar which is labelled POTTED SHRIMP but which really contains the remains of a cab-horse, you are committing a material sin by eating meat on a Friday, but you are not committing a formal sin, because you had no way of knowing that the cab-horse was there. And, of course, although you may mention it in confession if you find out about it afterwards, you are not *bound* to confess it, nor will it be brought up against you at the day of judgment; a sin does not lie upon your conscience unless you are conscious of committing it, and it is by your conscience that you will be judged. Similarly, the ordinary Englishman who has been validly baptized proceeds, later in life, to join in worship which is, as matter of fact, heretical and schismatical; but he is not blamed for it in the sight of God, because he has not, then at least, any means of finding out that he is doing so. The sin is merely a material one. Mark you, we no longer describe him as a Catholic; because we have to judge whether a person is or is not a Catholic by his outward actions. But has he ceased to be a member of the Mystical Body of Christ? No; not at least while he makes faithful use of the opportunities he has of worshipping God, according to the light given him. That means that there are quantities and quantities of people who, as far as we can determine, are already members of the Mystical Body of Christ *without knowing it*.

And now, how is it possible for such a person to lose that unconscious membership of Christ's Church? He can, of course, suspend the operation of grace, just as we Catholics can, if he commits mortal sin. On the other hand, he regains his lost state of grace if he makes an act of perfect contrition, just as a Catholic does. Only, whereas the Catholic is bound to make his sin known in confession, even though by God's grace it may already have been forgiven him, a Protestant is not so bound, because he either knows nothing about confession, or thinks that he can satisfy his obligation by confessing his sins to an Anglican clergyman, or to his friends in the groups. But there's another way in which he can lose his membership of the Mystical Body. He does so when the claims of the Catholic Church are fully proposed to him, and he sees that they are justified, but does not become a Catholic in spite of his knowledge. Pride, or indolence, or the hope of worldly advantage prevents him from taking the step which his conscience knows to be right. Then, in that hour, he becomes a heretic and a schismatic, formally as well as materially; he has refused grace.

Are there many people in that position? I don't know; my own impression is that there are very few Protestants who are Protestants in bad faith. They are in good faith, so long as they remain outside the Church through invincible ignorance. That's a phrase of ours that worries people frightfully; when we tell them they are the victims of invincible ignorance, they always look as if we had said something rude. But if you are arguing with a friend, and are driven to tell him in the last resort that invincible ignorance is what he is suffering from, don't let him go away with the impression that you are being rude, and that invincible ignorance means a sort of cretinous stupidity. If you've got a tutorial at six, and your watch tells you it's half-past five, and you're pretty sure your watch is wrong, and there's a clock in the next room you know to be right—then that ignorance of the time which makes you half an hour or so late for your tutorial is not invincible ignorance. It is vincible ignorance; you could have overcome it if you had taken the trouble to look at the clock in the next room. So your friend's ignorance would be vincible, if he already had a pretty shrewd idea that the Catholic position was right, but refused to read the C.T.S. tracts you offered him because he jolly well knew he was going to lose a legacy if he became a Catholic. But that's not his position; a hundred accidents of parentage, education, misconception, sentimental prejudice and so on make him so far from the Church that his conversion would seem a kind of miracle; he really knows nothing about Catholics except that you are one, which may or may not be an inducement—very well, his ignorance is invincible. It is the kind of ignorance he could not get rid of by taking any steps which he could normally be expected to take. So he's all right.

By now, as I well know, you are all bursting with an objection. It always crops up in these discussions. If (you say) this rosy picture of yours is true about the dispositions of

Protestants and their chances of eternal salvation, what exactly is the use of being a Catholic? Aren't Catholics, by your account of the matter, rather in the position of men who laboriously climb up the rugged slopes of a mountain, to find when they got to the top that their Protestant friends have got ahead of them by means of a funicular railway whose existence they themselves had never been taught to suspect? Here am I (you complain) tied down by all sorts of restrictions and regulations which interfere seriously with my enjoyment of the present life; and here are these Protestants, invincibly ignorant of all these rules and regulations, and therefore having all the fun which I miss, and no worse off when it comes to a future life than myself? Your attitude, in fact, is very much that of the labourers in the vineyard whom we read about in the Gospel, who complained that they had borne all the burden of the day and the heats, and at the end of it found themselves on exactly the same footing as the casual labourers who had been raked in from the market-place at the last moment.

Well, that opens up rather a large subject. You see, it isn't true that Protestants are exempt from the law of *God*, from the Ten Commandments for instance; and it isn't true that Protestants can be invincibly ignorant, to a full extent, of what God's law requires of them. Their consciences are doubtless confused; but don't be too ready to believe them when they say they see no harm in doing this or that which you know to be wrong. There's a very great deal of self-deception going about, when people say they "see no harm" in doing something they very much want to; it's not invincible ignorance when a man puts blinkers on his conscience. We are not to judge our Protestant friends in such cases; judgment lies with Almighty God, to whom each soul is responsible. But you mustn't think it true for a moment, or allow other people to think it true for a moment, that there is one Divine Law for Catholics and another for Protestants. However, that takes us away from our subject. Let us admit that where the law of the *Church* is concerned you are bound and your Protestant friends are not. They can do certain things which you can't do; they can eat a mutton-chop on a Friday, they can be Freemasons, they can get married in a registry office, they can leave directions in their wills to say they want to be cremated, and so on. From all these riotous pleasures you are excluded. And you want to know whether it isn't bad luck you should be excluded when they aren't. Or, putting the thing in a rather more altruistic way, why (you ask) should we bother to convert Protestants? Since they are in good faith, wouldn't it be better to leave them in good faith, and let them get to heaven in their own way, mutton-chops and all?

The immediate answer to that difficulty is this—that although we ought always to hope, for the sake of charity, that this or that Protestant is in good faith, we can't be sure that he is in good faith, nor, for that matter, can he. Therefore we should always encourage the conversion of a Protestant, if only for safety's sake. But, you know, even if you could be certain that some friend of yours was in good faith, and was on the whole a clean-living sort of person, so that there was no great reason to worry about him, it isn't true to say that you and he enjoy exactly the same supernatural advantages. First, you have the certainty of the faith; you are spared the anxious uncertainties which often assail him; he's not certain whether there is a future life, whether this life's worth living, whether anything you do or say really matters much—from those doubts you are set free. Second, you have access, where he has no access, to sacramental grace; he can win forgiveness for his sins (for example) only by an act of perfect contrition, and who can be certain that he is making an act of perfect contrition? Whereas for you attrition suffices, as long as you make use of the sacrament of penance. Third, you have the merits of the Church at your disposal; you can go out to Rome in the vac. and get a plenary indulgence, or (if your dispositions are not sufficient for that) an indulgence of some kind; he can go out to Kamschatka and he won't get off a day's Purgatory for it. The reason why you don't realize your privileges as Catholics is because you don't use them more.

As a matter of fact, even if there were no heaven and no hell, it would still be our duty to try and convert heretics, even those who are only in material heresy, for a different reason—that truth is truth, and has a right to be told. Spiritual truth, which is the highest of all, is something we must necessarily want to impart to other people if we possess it ourselves. I don't mean by that that I want you to go straight back to your College and try and convert the two people you are sitting next to in Hall. Indiscriminate attempts to convert other people mean, at the best, that you give people a dislike for Catholicism; at the worst, that you shake what faith they have in Christianity altogether, so that the last state of them is worse than the first. No, your duty is to defend the faith to the best of your power where you can see it is being misrepresented, and to help your friends when they begin to take an interest in the Catholic religion, by lending them books, by introducing them to a priest, or in some similar way.

There's one other point. If you are asked, "What is the exact meaning of the maxim, *No salvation outside the Catholic Church*," what are you to say about it? The simplest way to put it, I think, is this—there is no other religious body in the world except the Catholic Church which makes a supernatural contribution to a man's chances of salvation. He may receive natural help from some other source; his conscience may be stirred by the preaching of the Salvation Army, or he may learn a useful habit of mental prayer from the Buchmanites, or his sense of worship may be stimulated by the beauty of the ceremonies which he witnesses at the Church of the Cowley Fathers. But there's only one religious body whose membership, of itself, tends to procure our salvation, and that is the Catholic Church. If anybody is saved without visible membership of it he is saved, not because he's an Anglican, not because he's a Methodist, not because he's a Quaker, but for one reason only—because he is a Catholic without knowing it.

XIV

INTO ALL TRUTH

WHEN we say that the Church continues on earth the teaching work of her divine Founder, what picture are we to form in our minds of this, her teaching office? Are we to think of her as having received, once and for all, an inalienable and unalterable deposit of infallible doctrine, with no power to add to it, or take away from it, even to interpret it? Or are we to think of her as not only continuing to teach, but continuing to learn; as becoming aware, with the slow lapse of the centuries, of fresh truths, or at least fresh implications of the truth, so that the content of revelation does not remain static, but expands as the years go on, and promises an ever-increasing harvest of spiritual insight? Is the truth which the Church proclaims something which she has known all along, or something which she is gradually coming to know?

It is a curious point, which has not, I think, received the remark it deserves, that in the answer which it gives to that question Protestant theology has, within the last hundred years or so, completely boxed the compass. A hundred years ago, at the time when the Oxford Movement started, I think you can say that the vast majority of people in England who valued their reputation for orthodoxy—and at that date a great many people did—thought of Christian truth as a fixed body of doctrines which had always been held in the Church, and, lest they should be obscured through the lapse of time or through human subtlety, had all been written down somewhere or other in the books of the New Testament, too plain for anybody to miss them. The plain sense of Scripture—that is what they appealed to. Actually, of course, there is no plain sense of Scripture, and they were basing their tradition on the early fathers of the Church much more than they knew. But their appeal was always to the primitive, to the uncorrupted Church, and to the New Testament as the supreme test of what that Church taught.

For example, if you had asked in Protestant Oxford a hundred years ago whether eternal punishment existed in the next world, everybody, except perhaps a handful of dangerous liberals, would have replied, "Yes, of course." No matter whether you were High Church or Low Church, no matter whether you were Evangelical or Tractarian, you believed in eternal punishment because it was obviously the belief of the early Church, of the apostles, nay, of our Lord himself. Or again, if you had raised the question in Oxford a hundred years ago whether it was possible for a Christian to obtain a divorce in the full sense, to be rid of one marriage which had turned out unhappily, and free to marry again, the answer would have been an unmistakeable "No." What God hath joined, let not man put asunder; the wife is bound as long as her husband liveth—the New Testament was clear on the point; or, if there was a little confusion introduced by the difference of wording in St Matthew, the comments of the early fathers were enough to put that all right. The Christian tradition on the subject was clear, and the Church had nothing to do but to declare it. No new light could possibly be forthcoming on the subject; you would have to be a Quaker or an Anabaptist to suppose that it could.

Whereas, if you study any of the pronouncements of modern Protestant theology, you will find that its tone is exactly the opposite. It doesn't matter at what level you study the thing, whether in the careful pastorals of Anglican bishops or in the crude religiosity of the newspapers. Always you will get the impression that Christian theology is not something once for all delivered to the saints, and therefore fixed for all time; it is something which "the Church" is making up as it goes along. What precisely they mean by the Church it is not quite kind to enquire; but that is the assumption. "More and more we are coming to see that," "thoughtful Christians nowadays are at one in believing that," "modern speculation has no room for the mediæval idea that"—those are the rubrics under which religious truth is now presented to us. And there are half a dozen texts which are continually being quoted in support of such an attitude: "the Spirit shall guide you into all truth," "all thy people shall be taught of God," "he that doeth the works shall know the doctrine," and so on. We are learning all the time, these people would have us believe, in theology quite as much as in any other science; and you would no more expect St Thomas or John Calvin to have said the last word, for example, about the Holy Eucharist, any more than you would expect Boyle to have said the last word about gases, or Darwin about biology.

And when you put a concrete question to these Protestants of our own day, you feel far less certain as to what the answer will be. Some of them do still believe in the doctrine of eternal punishment, but most of them will tell you that we have given up believing in all that kind of thing *now*. Belief in eternal punishment was only a stage through which Christian thought had to pass; necessary perhaps to its development, but something which we have quite outgrown in these more enlightened days. The Church, which was once inspired by the Holy Ghost to believe in eternal punishment, has now received an even better inspiration from the Holy

Ghost to believe that there is no such thing. And even in practical matters, even over a question like divorce, you will find the same weakening process beginning to set in among the Protestant theologians; they want the innocent party at any rate to be dealt with mildly in such cases—quite oblivious of the fact that nowadays the innocent party is as a rule the guilty one. Mark you, I'm not talking only of the people who belong to the Modern Churchmen's Union. Quite High Church people, who regard themselves as the legitimate successors of the Tractarians, will tell you that Catholic truth is not a revelation which we possess already, but a revelation which is gradually being disclosed to us through the action of the Holy Spirit in the Church. The exact opposite of what they used to tell us a hundred years ago.

And then, of course, as so often happens when people have completely boxed the compass in their own thought, they turn on us and attack our position from an angle diametrically opposed to that from which we were hitherto accustomed to defend it. They used to say, I mean, a hundred years ago, "What blasphemous, superstitious, new-fangled people you Roman Catholics are, believing a whole lot of things which the early Church had never heard of, instead of sticking to the good, safe old ways! Your doctrine of the Immaculate Conception, for example—you went and introduced that in the middle of the nineteenth century; the early Fathers never mention it at all. Don't you realize that it is quite impossible for the Holy Ghost to tell us anything which he hasn't been telling us for the last nineteen hundred years?" And then, before we had finished telling them all about St Irenaeus and the doctrine of the second Eve, we suddenly found that the wind was blowing from another quarter, and we were being roundly abused for believing in the doctrine of original sin. "What stupid, pedantic, old-fashioned people you Roman Catholics must be," they were now saying, "believing a whole lot of nonsense which was believed by the early Church, as if everything stood still, and we hadn't learnt any lessons in theology since! This doctrine of original sin, for example—of course, it was good enough for the primitive, untutored minds of Irenaeus and his contemporaries; but you must surely realize that the Holy Ghost has been teaching us a lot of things since then? In particular, that the Fall wasn't really a fall; that the human race has been steadily developing upwards ever since its monkey days, and consequently the whole notion of original sin has to be set aside as a notion which was useful in its time, to express the limited theological ideas of the first ages, but is grotesquely antiquated now?" And so we had to start all over again, from a fresh angle.

Mr Belloc told me he was once walking with a friend in London, and they passed by a navvy who was digging up the road, and had paused to swear pretty freely at a bystander who had been rude to him. And Mr Belloc's friend said, "What an extraordinary thing it is that nine out of every ten Englishmen believe that that man was immaculately conceived!"

Well, what is *our* position about it all? Do we think of Catholic truth as something which has been revealed finally, once for all, when our Lord founded his Church? Or do we think of it as a growing body of truth, made known to us by successive revelations from the Holy Spirit, who has never ceased to dwell in and to energize his Church? The answer is that both those statements are true; and the harmonizing of those two statements is at once a very delicate and a very necessary piece of theological reasoning. We do believe that the whole of Christian truth was made known by our Lord to his apostles. Not, mark you, that it was all written down, fully at least, in the pages of the New Testament. We know from St Luke that our Lord, between his Resurrection and his Ascension, appeared to his disciples over a period of forty days, speaking to them of the things which concerned the kingdom of God. Only scattered fragments of that teaching remain on record; and yet, if you come to think of it, how closely the apostles must have questioned our Lord about all the theological issues which puzzled them; how carefully they must have treasured the words that fell from his lips, when he was so soon to leave them! It is chiefly, we must suppose, in the teaching of those forty days that the tradition of Christian doctrine, which has come down by unimpaired succession to our own days, is ultimately rooted. On the other hand, our Lord did promise that his Spirit should teach them all things, and bring all things to their remembrance, whatever he had said to them. Something, then, remained to be accomplished, if those early lessons were to take shape and achieve clearness of outline; if they were to maintain themselves against the altered conditions which later times would bring. The centuries, somehow, were to set their stamp on the deposit of faith. How exactly, and why exactly, did that happen?

The easiest way to understand it is perhaps by reference to the analogy of ordinary human law, and the way in which statute law grows in volume, and yet does not grow in extent, as successive decisions in case law define its meaning. Let us suppose, for example, that there is a law on the statute book—there may be, for all I know—that none of the King's subjects, except when he is on military service, may go about carrying weapons. There is a strict school of interpretation, which says that this law obviously forbids you to carry a walking-stick. Somebody is prosecuted for carrying a walking-stick, and acquitted. There is a lax school of interpretation, which says that, of course, there is no harm in carrying a carving-knife; that is not meant for wounding one's fellow-citizens, only for cutting up meat. A man is prosecuted for carrying a carving-knife, and condemned. Now, in a sense the law has grown in volume; there is more stuff to be read up in the legal textbooks. Instead of merely learning that the law does not allow men to carry weapons, you have to learn that the law does not allow men to carry carving-knives, but does allow men to carry walking-sticks. Yet the law has not really grown in extent; no addition has been made to it, nothing has been subtracted from it. All that has happened is that the law has been interpreted, in the sense in which it was obviously meant to be interpreted; its scope has not been extended, but its meaning has been more accurately defined.

So it is that Christian theology grows, and yet does not grow, with the centuries. Somebody produces an explanation of some Christian doctrine which is obviously a disingenuous explanation, an attempt to explain it away. There is friction and debate; perhaps a rival school grows up which threatens, by reaction, to overstate the case on the other side. Then, if the disputants on either side stick obstinately to their opinions, the Church is called upon to define the issue; and in doing so she invokes the aid of the Holy Spirit, asking him to guide her into all truth; asking him to remind her what exactly it was our Lord taught her, in those distant days by the sea of Galilee. And when she has framed her definition, the truth of Christian doctrine remains what it was; nothing has been added to it, nothing has been subtracted from it. But it has grown in clearness; what was once held by the faithful as a confused truth stands out more luminous, has sharper edges; in that sense, Christian theology has been enriched.

It is not difficult to choose examples which will illustrate that principle. Let me speak of two which we shall be commemorating only a few days from now.

The earliest Christians knew well enough that the Divine Nature was single, indivisible, and unique; to say that there were two Gods or three Gods would be blasphemy, a relapse into paganism. On the other hand, they believed firmly in

God the Father, like the Jews before them; they believed that our Lord Jesus Christ was God; and they believed that the Holy Spirit, sent to them from both, was God. I will pray the Father, and he will send you another Comforter—three Persons are in question there. On the other hand, I and the Father are one—somehow, Trinity and Unity are reconcilable. Then came the age of the great heresies; Arius tried to explain away the mystery by denying the Godhead of Christ; Macedonius, by denying the Godhead of the Holy Spirit; Sabellius, by making out that the distinction between the Father, the Son, and the Holy Spirit was only a distinction of functions or aspects. So it was that the Church had to call to her aid philosophical distinctions, hitherto unfamiliar; she could only safeguard the truth once for all delivered to her against sophistical interpretation by making a new definition; there were three Persons in the Godhead, but only one Divine Substance. She did not alter her belief, or add to it, or abandon anything of it; she only sharpened the sword of truth to give it a keener edge against error.

That was only three or four centuries after Christ; the doctrine of the Holy Eucharist remained much longer in its unformed state, because theologians had not yet arisen to exercise their subtleties on it. There could be no doubt at all that what the priest held in his hands was the Body of Christ, that what the Chalice contained was the Blood of Christ; he himself had said so, who could neither deceive nor be deceived. Yet there was no doubt that what the priest held retained the appearance of bread, that what was in the Chalice still looked and still tasted like wine; you could not deny the evidence of your own senses. The two truths must be held together, as mysteriously coexisting. Then, at last, attempts were made to explain away the doctrine by supposing that the words of Institution were only symbolic, that no real change was effected when the consecration took place.

5*

And once more the Church had to make use of philosophical distinctions which till then had not seemed necessary; to explain that what was present was the very substance of our Lord's Body and Blood, although the accidents proper to bread and wine remained unaltered. Once more, there was no addition, no alteration; after the fourth Lateran Council as before it the Church held the faith which her Master had delivered to her; only she held it in more precise terms, only with less risk, henceforward, of being misrepresented or misunderstood.

When we say, then, that the teaching of the Church is the teaching of Christ, we mean two things. In the first place, that the substance of what we assert comes down to us, by continuous tradition, from his own teaching given to his apostles. In the second place that the formulæ in which our belief is enshrined are the only true interpretation of his meaning, guaranteed to us by his promise that his Holy Spirit would guide the Church into all truth.

XV

THE KEY MAN

THE Council of Trent, although its delibera-
tions are portentous in their bulk, and occupy
just one-tenth of the whole number of pages
in Denzinger's *Handbook of the Creeds and
Definitions of the Church*, didn't discuss the
question of the Pope's primacy at all. In spite of all the trouble
with the mediæval councils, in spite of all the bitter attacks
made by Luther and the Reformers upon the Papacy, the
Council of Trent didn't think it worth while to enter into
the subject, except for five lines, no more than five lines, in
the short profession of faith which it issued. "I recognize that
the Catholic and Apostolic church at Rome is the mother and
mistress of all churches, and I promise and swear obedience
to the Roman bishop, the successor of blessed Peter (Chief
of theApostles) and Vicar of Jesus Christ." That was all that
was said; that was all that needed to be said. Protestants often
talk as if the Church of Rome dated from the Council of
Trent; as if the real breach in continuity between the
primitive Church and the modern Roman Church happened
just there. And yet the doctrine of the Pope's primacy, which
is the real issue between us and them, wasn't discussed at the
Council; it was simply pushed away into a corner as something no reasonable man would dream of disputing. In other
words, it was there already.

Another curious point is this—you would naturally have

imagined that after all the upheaval of the sixteenth century, when Europe as a whole had had to make up its mind whether it would remain Catholic or turn Protestant, there could be no more fuss and no more question over the position of the Roman Pontiff. You would have thought that difficulty settled once for all. Yet, as a matter of fact, one of the bitterest attacks ever made on the position of the Pope—though it is true it only attacked certain of his privileges and attacked them in a limited sort of way—happened between the Council of Trent in the sixteenth century and the Council of the Vatican in the nineteenth century; in fact you may say that its influence was at work in a more or less degree all through that period. This attack was the movement or theological tendency, perhaps it is best to call it a tendency, known as Gallicanism.

Fundamentally, Gallicanism was a difference of opinion between France and the rest of Catholic Europe as to certain "liberties" claimed by the French Church as a local Church. The liberties were not really liberties at all, they were the claims of an absolute monarch to interfere in Church affairs, particularly in the matter of appointing to vacant sees, and in the still more lucrative matter of appropriating the revenues of the sees while they were vacant. During the latter half of the seventeenth century, in the great period of Louis XIV, relations between Catholics in France and the Holy See were very much what relations between Catholics in England and the Holy See had been in the great days of Henry VIII, between 1530 and 1550. It really looked as if Louis was not content with saying *L'état, c'est moi*, and wanted to be able to say *L'église, c'est moi* as well. Humanly speaking, you might have anticipated that the history of sixteenth-century England might have repeated itself in seventeenth-century France, if Louis XIV had happened to want a divorce. Fortunately he didn't, he wasn't much interested in that sort of thing. And by the end of the seventeenth century Gallicanism as a political danger had come to an end. But it remained as a tendency, and a very formidable tendency, right up to the time of the French Revolution and beyond it.

You see, Gallicanism didn't stop short at claiming certain liberties for the Church in France. It had, at least in its extreme form, an attitude of its own about the relation between the authority of Popes and the authority of general councils. It deliberately reaffirmed the decrees promulgated at the Council of Constance, but never accepted by the Church, which asserted that a general council has an authority superior to that of the Pope. All through history absolute monarchs have been fond of general councils. It is very difficult for an absolute monarch to get hold of the Pope and make him say what he wants him to say; it is not very difficult for him, if his territories are sufficiently wide, to collect an assemblage of carefully chosen bishops and make *them* say what he wants them to say. That was how Arianism so long survived its condemnation at Nicea. That was really how the Eastern dioceses grew away from, and finally split away from, their Catholic unity with the Church of the West. Louis XIV believed in absolute monarchy, and consequently he believed in general councils. And the general effect of Gallicanism was to spread, in those countries which came under French influence, the topsy-turvy and quite unworkable notion that the Pope's decrees, whatever their solemnity, are not irreformable, and consequently cannot be regarded as infallible, until they have been ratified by the consent of the Church—normally, that is, by the vote of a general council.

You might have thought that all this questioning of the papal prerogative would have found no echo in England, where for a century and more martyrs had bled in defence of the papacy. But as a matter of fact we English Catholics are intimately concerned with the history of Gallicanism. You must remember that from the time of James II onwards whatever political hopes Catholics could have were centred in France. You must remember that most of our clergy had been trained in France, and that the books of piety we used were largely imported from France. And the result was that when a Committee of Catholic gentlemen, in the year 1879, drew up a Protestation on behalf of the English Catholics stating what they really believed, and later a form of oath which they were prepared to accept as the condition of being emancipated from their civil disabilities, that protestation and that oath contained the extraordinary words, "We acknowledge no infallibility in the Pope."

That fact is sure to be quoted against us next year, when we celebrate the centenary of our complete emancipation, which, of course, followed some time later. We shall be reminded, as Mr Gladstone reminded us at the time of the Vatican Council, that we really obtained emancipation under false pretences, by declaring our readiness to disown a doctrine which has subsequently become a defined doctrine of the Church. It is important, then, to examine the circumstances of the time a little. In the first place, the four bishops who then acted as Vicars Apostolic in England only consented to sign the protestation when it was explained to them that the whole paragraph was only meant to apply to the Pope's interference in temporal matters, and did not limit his authority in things ecclesiastical; that this had been the undoubted intention of those by whom the protestation was drawn up. In the second place, it is to be remembered that the oath was not signed by the bishops, and indeed was twice condemned by the bishops, though their grounds for doing so were never fully made clear. And in the third place, the oath was never actually taken. Providence interfered, through the rather unlikely agency of the Anglican Bishop of St David's, and the emancipation granted in 1791 was secured to Catholics on condition of their taking a quite unobjectionable oath, similar to that which had already been employed for the same purpose in Ireland.

With all that, I think you can't deny that our ancestors—and I may say that some of your ancestors were badly mixed up in it—were sailing very close to the wind. They weren't guilty of formal heresy, but they did propose to correct the faith of eighteen centuries to suit the policy of a *côterie* of squires gathered in a coffee-house. If the counsels of the Committee had prevailed, we English Catholics should certainly have looked very foolish after the findings of the Vatican Council in 1870.

That Council was not convened to discuss the subject of infallibility. It was convened to discuss questions arising out of the new attitude of Liberalism, in politics and in thought, with which the world seemed to have become permeated since the French Revolution. The discussion of infallibility was introduced into the agenda as the result of representations made by various bishops in different parts of the world—for example, the Archbishop of Baltimore. It was almost inevitable that the question should arise. On the one hand, the Gallican influence was not yet dead. On the other hand, a new and active school of ultramontanes had come into existence, represented by Veuillot in the *Univers* and W. G. Ward in the *Dublin Review*. Reacting from Gallicanism, these writers appeared determined to exaggerate the privileges of the papacy at the expense of bishops and of councils; they wanted even the casual utterances of the Holy Father to be invested with infallibility, and Ward, it is well known, said he would like to have an infallible definition served up every morning with his breakfast. These two schools were growing so violently apart that it would have been impossible to summon an ecumenical council without canvassing their differences.

The question raised at the Council was not whether the Pope was infallible, everybody admitted that; but, first, whether the moment was opportune for deciding the matter —hence the opposition were called "inopportunists"—and, second, what were the attendant conditions which made a papal decree recognizably infallible. In the event, the Cisalpine party was defeated in the sense that a decree *was* passed by the Council. It was passed by 433 votes to 2; though by that time a good many bishops had withdrawn, some by way of protesting that the decree was inopportune, some for the more practical reason that France was just going to war with Germany. In any case, it was a clear majority of the bishops who attended the Council from first to last—roughly four in seven. On the other hand, the wording in which the decree was drafted may more reasonably be considered a defeat for the ultramontanes, since it refuses to extend the limits of infallibility precisely where the ultramontanes would have wished to extend them.

The decree states that "when the Roman pontiff speaks *ex cathedra* (that is, when he decides, in the exercise of his office as shepherd and teacher of all Christians, by virtue of his supreme Apostolic authority, that a doctrine concerning faith or morals is to be held by the entire Church), he possesses, in consequence of the divine aid promised him in St Peter, that infallibility with which the Divine Saviour wished his Church to be endowed, for the definition of doctrine concerning faith or morals; and that such definitions of the Roman pontiff are of themselves, and not in consequence of the Church's consent, irreformable."

Now, it's true that that last phrase deals Gallicanism its death blow. It gets rid for ever of the quite unworkable idea that the authority of the Pope depends on the authority of the Council. There is no way of deciding which councils were ecumenical councils except by saying that those councils were ecumenical which had their decisions ratified by the Pope. Now, either that ratification is infallible of itself, or else you will immediately have to summon a fresh ecumenical council to find out whether the Pope's ratification was infallible or not, and so on *ad infinitum*. You can't keep on going round and round in a vicious circle; in the long run the last word of decision must lie with one man, and that man is obviously the Pope. In the last resort the Pope must be the umpire, must have the casting vote. If therefore there is to be any infallibility in the Church, that infallibility must reside in the Pope, even when he speaks in his own name, without summoning a council to fortify his decision. So far, the definition was a triumph, if you will, for the ultramontanes. But all the rest of the language in which the decree is couched is very careful language, clearly designed to show that the Pope is not always infallible, but only in certain special conditions—and those conditions so elaborately expressed, that there can be no doubt of the Council's general intention to limit the sphere of infallibility.

Gallicanism is dead; it has, by a curious process of history, committed suicide. Its argument was that whereas the Pope is fallible a general council is infallible. Now, there is no question that the Vatican Council was a general council, from the point of view of the Catholic Church; its decrees were fully accepted by all those bishops who did not actually sign them, without a single dissentient. Therefore the Vatican Council is infallible, and when it says that the Pope is infallible, that statement is infallibly true. If, then, Gallican-like, you believe in the infallibility of general councils, you have to believe in the infallibility of the Pope as well. That situation was admirably summed up by the Bishop of Little Rock, an American bishop who had been one of the two dissentients at the Council. "Holy Father," he said, "*now* I believe." He had to; we all have to. You may be a Catholic now, or you may be an Anglican, but you cannot be a Gallican any more.

There have been great men, and good men, and honest men, all through the history of the Church who have felt scruples about the exercise of the papal prerogative and the direction in which it was tending, from St Cyprian down to Cardinal Newman. But in every age the general sense of the faithful has resisted any suspicion of an attempt to democratize the constitution of the Church in defiance of our Lord's promises. As you all know, at the final sitting of the Vatican Council, when the infallibility question was decided, a terrific thunderstorm broke over Rome. And the Council was itself a thunderstorm; it cleared the air. The Church has had plenty of troubles to meet since 1870, and plenty of difficulties to solve; but the old dispute between Cisalpines and Ultramontanes, which so tragically separated Veuillot and Dupanloup, Ward and Newman, has passed into the region of forgotten controversies. And the rock of Peter stands unshaken, only with a fresh definition as a fresh high-water mark to show where the last flood reached.

XVI

VERBUM CARO FACTUM EST

OUR Lord Jesus Christ was both God and Man. As you all know, the formula in which Catholic theology enshrines that notion, the polish which Catholic theology gives to that rough jewel of truth, is the formula of the Hypostatic Union. We all learned to repeat those words before we had the foggiest notion what they meant; they tripped so easily off our tongues that the first word got shortened down into *haipstatic*, and perhaps became vaguely connected in our minds with the meaningless sort of shout we used to hear on the parade ground. However, we know a little more about it now; at least I hope we do. The doctrine of the hypostatic union is that in the historical figure of Jesus of Nazareth we have to distinguish two natures, a human and a divine Nature; but that those two natures belong to a single Person, and that Person is wholly divine.

Well, you say, when we've got as far as that we haven't really got much further. After all, what do we know about what is meant by the word Nature, or what is meant by the word Person? Aren't we defining something which is obscure by something more obscure still, and isn't that a fallacy of elementary logic? Well, of course, there is a certain amount of truth in that criticism. Our minds can't fully grasp the meaning of obscure notions like nature and person even when we are dealing with ordinary human subjects of study; much less then, when we are talking about God, to whose Being our human language only implies imperfectly. But at the same time, we are not to suppose that the Fathers of the Church taught us to talk about nature and person merely so as to plunge us into a condition of pious confusion; like the old Protestant lady in the story, who said what a lot of comfort she got out of that blessed word Mesopotamia. No, theological language is meant to make the mysteries of our religion not more obscure than they were, but on the contrary a little more precise, and a little more accurately defined than they were. It is designed, not exactly to make the thing easier to believe, but to make it easier to know what exactly we are called upon to believe in.

And in order to understand that language, much the simplest recipe is to make a little excursion into Church history, and see what heresies it was—or rather, what errors it was, for an error does not become a heresy until it is contrary to defined truth—that these definitions were meant to warn us against. One hears that tramps have a special sign which they chalk up on the walls of a house which means, "No good trying here; you won't get anything out of that." I always wish I knew what it was, because one could buy a piece of chalk and save oneself a deal of trouble. In the same sort of way, the Church, who has centuries of experience behind her, chalks up, as it were, on certain lines of theological explanation, "No good trying here, you won't get anything out of that." And the negative warnings which she gives us when she anathematizes errors can be stated, if you will, as positive warnings instead, and it is these positive warnings which you will find expressed in her creeds.

God is one, God is three—that is all the early Church knew about the doctrine of the Trinity, and all it needed to know. It was only when people started trying to be clever and to explain the doctrine of the Trinity by formulæ which really had the effect of explaining *away* the doctrine of the Trinity, that closer definition became necessary. Somebody, for example, would try to make the doctrine a little easier for people outside to understand by explaining that when you talked about God the Father, God the Son, and God the Holy Ghost, you were simply talking about the same Divine Person under three different aspects, looking at him from three different points of view. And then the Catholic bishops would ask themselves, "Does that really express the doctrine which was handed down to me by my predecessors, and to them by the holy apostles?" And the moment they asked themselves that question, the reply was obvious, "No, I'm hanged if it does." So they had to get together and hammer out a formula which would make it clear that, whatever the doctrine of the Trinity meant, it certainly meant something different from that, a something more important than that, something more mysterious than that. And so they insisted that, although the Godhead is a single thing, the distinction between the Father, the Son, and the Holy Ghost is a real distinction between persons, not a mere distinction of thought between three different aspects of the same thing. Or again, right up to the later part of the Dark Ages the Church was content to say, when she was called upon to express her Eucharistic doctrine, that the bread and wine became, in the Mass, the Body and Blood of Christ. It was only eight centuries or so after Christ that the controversies began which had to be settled, in the end, by defining the doctrine of Transubstantiation. And the language about substance and accidents which is now so familiar to us had to be applied to the problem in order that the incomplete, insincere explanations of Eucharistic doctrine which had then been invented might be seen to be incomplete and insincere. So with the Infallibility of the Pope; Catholics had simply been content to believe that the charisma of infallibility was vested in the see which had been founded by Peter, without enquiring any more closely what were the conditions of its exercise. It wasn't till after the Counter-Reformation, when the Gallicans produced their half-hearted explanations of what it meant, that it became necessary to define the doctrine in terms which would make such error impossible in future; and that, as we know, was done as late as the year 1870.

And so it is with this doctrine of our Lord's Incarnation. That he was believed from the very earliest times to be both God and Man is the only possible explanation of the language which the Church, from the very earliest times, has used about him. But it wasn't till more than three centuries after his death that it became necessary to speculate in what sense he could be both God and Man at the same time. And that was because people began to produce explanations of the mystery which, consciously or unconsciously, were dishonest explanations. They got rid of the mystery by exaggerating the doctrine in one direction or the other; either by treating our Lord as God in a way which meant that he was not really Man, or by treating him as Man in a way which meant that he was not really God.

On the one side, you could talk and write as if his Manhood had been altogether swallowed up in his Godhead. The extremest form which that kind of speculation took was the form known as Docetism; the notion that he was God all the time and merely took on the *appearance* of a Man. There was a difficulty, to be sure; if he was not really Man, how did he come to die on the Cross? The Docetists were reduced, apparently, to the supposition that at the last moment he simply withdrew from the earth, and allowed some man—I think they even suggested that it was Simon of Cyrene—to be crucified in his stead. That sort of theology was evidently too fantastic to catch on much. But, short of that, you might hold that our Lord in becoming Incarnate took upon him a true human *Body*, so that he was able to suffer and to die, but not a complete human *Nature*, in the sense of having human feelings, a human intellect, a human will. The second Person of the Blessed Trinity, in the totality of his spiritual Nature, simply replaced, in the Man Jesus Christ, all the spiritual part of man; that gave you a nice simple explanation of the whole story, though to be sure it was difficult to see how God Incarnate in this sense could be said to grow in wisdom and knowledge; or how our Lord could pray in Gethsemane that God's Will might be done, not his, when in fact on the hypothesis we are considering he had no will which was not Divine. From this explanation, anyhow, the whole instincts of Catholic orthodoxy recoiled. The Incarnate, so interpreted, might have a human Body, but not a true human Nature. "No," said the Church, "there are two Natures in Christ, not one."

On the other side, with Nestorius, you could so over-emphasize our Lord's sacred Humanity as to make it appear that he was not in the true sense God, but only a Man indwelt by the Presence of God to a unique degree and perhaps in a unique manner. You could speak as if the Child which was born of our Blessed Lady was just an ordinary human child such as you and I were once; the Nestorians, as you probably know, would not refer to our Lady as the Mother of God, for that reason; and the title of Theotokos became, at the time of the Nestorian controversy, a kind of touchstone of orthodoxy. At some time in his life, perhaps even as late as his Baptism, when the cloud was seen overshadowing him, the second Person of the Blessed Trinity came down and dwelt in this Man Christ Jesus, uniting himself to the Man Jesus Christ, by a union closer, of course, than any union which has ever been experienced by the greatest of his saints. And this explanation, too, the Church rejects as unsatisfactory. "No," she says, "that's not the primitive meaning of the language used in the very earliest Christian documents about the Incarnation. If it were anything so comparatively simple as all that, why should anybody have bothered to make it more complicated? The very plausibility of your theory shows that it's wrong—that it's a modern variant, an attempt to explain the thing away. If the baby who lay in the manger at Bethlehem was not, then and there, Almighty God, then that baby was a human person. And the second Person of the Blessed Trinity is also a Person; so that in your Incarnation you have to make use of a highly unphilosophic conception, that of two Persons becoming literally one. No, there are two Natures in the Incarnate, not just one; but at the same time there is only one Person in the Incarnate, not two."

The Christian mysteries transcend human thought. But they do not contradict human thought; they cut across our experience just at those points where it is impossible to say "This or that is impossible" because human thought, even in interpreting ordinary human experience, finds in it, at those points, an insoluble mystery. The Christian mysteries grow, as it were, out of the chinks in our armour of thought, just as a flower will grow, not out of a wall but out of a chink in the wall. Take the mystery of Transubstantiation. Impossible, you say, that the substance of a thing should be changed into a different substance while the accidents remain unaltered. No, you have no right to say that that is impossible; because the whole relation between substance and accidents is itself a kind of natural mystery; it is a thing which eludes our thought. Think of an orange; it is of a yellow colour, more or less round in shape, about two and half inches across, has a particular, well-defined smell, often met with in railway carriages. Yes, but what *is* the orange? Are we to think of it as a kind of hatstand on which this yellowness, this roundness, these two and half inches of diameter, this pungent smell, are hung up like so many hats? You are up against the whole puzzle of the relation of universals to particulars, which people have wrangled about for more than twenty centuries, and still haven't arrived at a unanimous conclusion. It is just there, just where "the wheeling systems darken, and our benumbed conceiving soars" that a Voice comes in from the other world and says "This is my Body."

Or again, take the mystery of grace and free will. How, you ask, can one and the same action at one and the same time be God's action and mine? It's impossible. But no, you see; once again we have come across one of these chinks, as I call them, in the armour of human thought. It is true that the relation of grace to free will is a mystery; but then, free will itself is a mystery, which defies all explanation, and when you think you have come across an explanation of it you find that, after all, you have left the facts out of account. Take a merely frivolous case in which, to all appearances at least, the faculty of human choice is exercised. You want to buy a new tie, and you have to choose between a green tie and a brown one. What happens when you choose? Are the attractions of the brown tie so irresistible that they compel you to buy it instead of the other? If so, it is not you who have chosen the brown tie, it is the brown tie that has chosen you. Or do you make up your mind as between the green tie and the brown tie independently of the attractions or the suitability of either? In that case you have not *chosen*, you have merely tossed up, so to speak, in your mind, and it is chance, not you, that has selected the brown one. In every act of choice there is a mystery staring you in the face—the mystery of that process by which your will identifies itself with a motive. And it's just at that point, where our thought inevitably flounders in any case, that the Divine action comes into our lives; it is God that gives us both to think and to do of his good pleasure.

And it's the same with this mystery of the hypostatic union. It's all nonsense, you complain, to talk about "person" and "nature" as if they were two quite separate things; as if you could stick a nature on to a person just as you stick a postage stamp on to an envelope. That is crude, mediæval psychology; we know more about that sort of thing nowadays. Yes, but if you come right down to it, what *do* we know about that sort of thing nowadays? When you turn your thought inwards, and think about yourself, who is thinking about whom, or what is thinking about what? You are not simply thinking about your thought about yourself; because that would mean that you were thinking about your thought about your thought about your thought about yourself and so on *ad infinitum*. No, the term of your thought is *you*, the person who is thinking. And in doing so, you have already divided yourself up, in a sense, into two; the intellectual nature which is thinking, and the person, somehow mysteriously connected with that intellectual nature, who is being thought about. No, we don't really know anything about the relations between a person and a nature; we've come up against yet another of those gaps in our thought, where the soil of natural mystery gives room for the flower of supernatural mystery to blossom. When our Lord thought about himself, the intellectual nature which thought was human; the Person who was being thought about was not human, but divine. That is mystery, if you like; but it is mystery in clear-cut terms.

And don't forget the difference between natural mystery and supernatural mystery. When we come up against a natural mystery, it's an uncomfortable sort of experience; we feel inclined to apologize for it, to be ashamed of it. Here is the whole world around me full of accidents and of substances, full, that is, of sense-impressions which I can't deny, and which can't nevertheless be the whole of reality, and I can't for the life of me find out what the relation between a substance and its accidents is! Here am I continually making choices, moral choices or choices of convenience, and I can't even determine the relation between my will and the motives which influence it; here am I dignified, as a human being, with the power of self-conscious thought, and yet whenever I think about myself I'm hanged if I know what it is I'm thinking about. It's a perpetual irritation to an intellectual creature to be coming up against blank walls all the time; and that's why philosophers always look worried. But with a *supernatural* mystery, which comes in at just these same points and makes them more mysterious than ever, we are not meant to feel ashamed of ourselves; we are not meant to apologize. No, we say, "Hullo, another mystery! Splendid! That's fine! Now the supernatural is really getting to work, the two sides of the mystery, the positive and negative poles as it were, effecting a discharge. That's all right; that is what we were expecting!"

You see, these people who produce ingenious explanations by way of making the Christian mysteries easier for our thought, only do it at the expense of spoiling the story. The Christian faith derives its interest, after all, from two decisive moments in our Lord's life—Bethlehem and Calvary. Consider how poor a story you make of Bethlehem if you believe, with the Nestorian, that there were two Persons in the Incarnation, the second Person of the Blessed Trinity and the person of a man Jesus Christ. In that case, the child in the manger is simply an ordinary human child who is destined, one day, to be mysteriously overshadowed by the Presence of God. But that's not the story; the point of the story is that the Child in the Manger *was* God. Or consider how poor a story you make of Calvary if, with the Monophysite, you believe that there was only one nature in the Incarnation, and that nature divine. Oh, no doubt as long as our Lord had a human Body the physical sufferings of Calvary were real. But the mental sufferings, the disappointment, the disillusionment, the fear, the grief over Judas' treachery and Peter's denial, the offering, in Gethsemane, of the human will to the divine—all that goes, all that becomes unreal, unless you believe that our Lord had a true human Nature which could be the seat of all those emotions. Once again, that's not the story; the story is that while he who suffered was God, he suffered with all the anguish, mental as well as physical, which belongs to the nature of Man.

So don't let's think that when the Church teaches us the doctrine of the hypostatic union she is merely using long words for the sake of using long words, merely trying to confuse us. It's not that at all; she is trying to safeguard, as accurately as human language can safeguard, the essential truth of the Incarnation; she only wants to make us realize that when she says God became Man she is not guilty of a metaphor or a piece of pulpit rhetoric. God did really become Man; was Man, and lay in the manger, was Man, and hung on the Cross, is Man, and has united with himself for ever that human nature he took, humiliated on earth, scarred with the scars of earth; reigns in it, eternally, in heaven.

XVII

ET HABITAVIT IN NOBIS

THE Incarnation of our Lord is a mystery. And wherever it deals with mystery, you will find that Catholic theology is a middle way between two extremes. That is natural, because a theological mystery always involves something which seems to our minds a contradiction; we are expected to hold simultaneously two truths which are apparently irreconcilable. And there is an obvious temptation for the incomplete theologian, when he is up against that kind of situation, to explain away one of those truths in the interests of the other. It's like cheating at patience, one can see in a moment that it is wrong, because it makes the thing too simple. So here, in the mystery of the Incarnation. Fr D'Arcy, I expect, told you last Sunday about Nestorianism and those more modern views, all tainted with Nestorianism, which explain away the mystery of the Incarnation by explaining away the statement that our Lord was God. This morning, we have to deal with the opposite error; with the ideas of the Docetæ, and Apollinarians, and Monophysites, and Monothelites, who tried to explain away the mystery of the Incarnation by explaining away the statement that our Lord was Man.

If you are in the habit of arguing about theology with your non-Catholic friends, you have probably discovered that about 90 per cent. of them don't believe our Lord was God. They say they do, lots of them; they think they do, but they've got it all wrong; they only mean that our Lord was a Man morally united, in will and purpose, to God. And if you succeed in persuading one of them that that is all wrong, that our Lord was *personally* God, you will probably find that he has fallen straight into the opposite pitfall. "Oh, you mean he was really God disguised under the outward appearance of a Man? Rather like Transubstantiation?" No, that won't do; that's Docetism. "Oh, I see; then you mean that he had the body of a man, but his soul was Divine?" No, that won't do either; that's Apollinarianism. "Then I suppose you mean our Lord had a human Nature to start with, but when the Incarnation happened, the Divine Nature came and swamped it, so to speak; it wasn't recognizably human any longer?" No, that's Monophysitism. The Christian doctrine of the Incarnation is that a single Person, the second Person of the Blessed Trinity, had, and has, two distinct natures at the same time. The Person of the Divine Word, and the Person of the Man, Jesus of Nazareth, are one and the same.

When we've said that, we've done something. We've made it clear what the hypostatic union is *not*. You know how, going up and down the river, you sometimes come across a stone monument telling you where somebody or other was drowned. It's nice that he should have a memorial; it is also a good thing that you should be told which parts of the river are treacherous to bathe in. And the creeds are like those monuments; when you've seen where Apollinaris fell in, and where Nestorius fell in, and where Eutyches fell in, you don't, unless you're a fool, go and make the same mistake. The Church has put up signposts—traffic-lights which you gate-crash at your peril. You know what Catholic doctrine isn't. But, on the positive side, when you've said that two Natures were united under a single Person, you haven't made the truth more luminous to your own mind. We don't know what a Person is, and we don't know what a nature is. All you can say, quite roughly, is that your nature is what you have, and your person is what you are. When a burglar is arrested, you sometimes read that so many bank notes were found on his person. They weren't really, of course; they were found in his clothes; and if you take off your clothes, your person is still there. And when your soul is separated from your body at death, your person will still be there, in your soul. But your soul isn't a bare personality; it has a nature; has memory, intellect, and will. If you lose your memory, you are still the same person; you can be sent to prison for an offence which you committed before you lost your memory. Your person is something underlying that memory, that intellect, that will; it is an idea so subtle that we can only reach it by abstraction. Philosophy has to confess itself beaten when it is asked what it means by the distinction between the person, what a man is, and the nature, what a man has; it's a mystery of our common human thought. And out of that mystery grows the mystery of the hypostatic union.

That being so, we must be careful how we think of our Lord in his Incarnate state. We must remember that the nature he took upon himself at the Incarnation was human, not divine. And, therefore, when a person says, "I can't understand how our Lord, if he was God, could be tempted in the wilderness, or agonize in the Garden, or feel dereliction on the Cross, or how he grew in wisdom and knowledge," he is stating the problem wrongly. There is a problem, but he is stating it wrongly. We don't know enough about the relations between person and nature to be able to say how much and in what manner the divineness of our Lord would overflow, so to speak, into his human experience. It was his *human* nature that was tempted, and agonized; it was as Man, not as God, that he learnt his alphabet. You've no apparatus, here, for deciding that such and such an experience was impossible to him.

But, as I say, there is a problem. Because it is the tradition of Catholic theology that our Lord, even as Man, possessed all the highest qualities of which a human nature is capable, where those qualities would not be inconsistent with the purpose which the Incarnation had in view. Thus, they teach that our Lord was not subject to disease, because disease is an imperfection; but at the same time he was capable of suffering —of thirst, for example, or weariness—because suffering was an essential part of his mission on earth. Human nature, after all, is made in the image of God; and our Lord, even as Man, was God-like as far as it is possible for man to be so; except where that would be inconsistent with his mission, with the character of that suffering Servant who came to redeem man by his obedience, and his exposure to misfortune. And that involves some important and at first sight disconcerting consequences.

Let's look at it in this way. There are three perfections in God which it is easy for us to recognize, if only because they contrast so glaringly with our own imperfections. Christ as God is all-powerful, is all-wise, is all-good. Was Christ as Man all-powerful, all-wise, all-good? If not, what limitations were imposed on him, and on what principle?

Was Christ as Man all-powerful, in the sense that his physical powers knew no limits, that his endurance was inexhaustible, his muscular strength unlimited? Clearly not. Such qualities do not contribute to the perfection of human nature; we have no reason to think they existed in Adam, for instance. And if they had existed in our Lord, then he could not have been hungry or thirsty or tired, as he evidently was. I think it is consoling to reflect that this would apply not only to his purely physical strength, but to his nervous resources as well. When you think of the life which he led on earth, do not think only of his bodily fatigue, think of the nervous strain it must have been—all those multitudes flocking round him, how tired we get of crowds! All those stupid questions he was asked—how tired we get of stupid questions! The shortness of the career which he allowed himself, three years, less than three years really, to convert a world—how exhausting it is, working always against time! In all this he would share our disabilities; he would hallow, beforehand, our worst experiences. And in Gethsemane he reached, and allowed us to see his reaching, the extremity of nervous humiliation. There was a sense, you see, in which our Lord was actually afraid of death. You may know the story of a Spanish general who showed nervousness on the eve of battle, and was asked, "Surely, General, you are not afraid?" To which his answer was, "Sir, my body is afraid of the dangers into which my spirit is going to lead it." That is, partly, the meaning of our Lord's agony. His body was afraid of the dangers into which his spirit was going to lead it.

But, you see, there is a different sense in which we might ask whether our Lord, as Man, was all-powerful. Had he control, if he would, over the forces of nature, so that he could bend them to his will? And the answer to that, I suppose, is that he could not do that, precisely as Man; but, all the time he was Man, he was also God. Such authority over the winds and the sea, over disease and death, belonged to his Person rather than to his Nature; and his Person was Divine. Jesus of Nazareth, therefore, performed miracles in virtue of his own dignity; and his human nature was an instrument in performing them. And here, I think, you may observe two indications of our Lord's condescension, his courtesy. In the first place, although his Godhead has always the right to command, he prefers to show us his Humanity at prayer. Just before that tremendous moment when he stood outside the tomb and cried, "Lazarus, come forth!" he said—what? "Father, I give thee thanks that thou hast heard me." He would sooner we thought of him as the *instrumental* cause

6

through which God does miracles than as the *agent* who does miracles himself. That ought to teach us, oughtn't it, to throw ourselves into the background rather more than we do? And there's a second point about our Lord's use of his superhuman powers—whether as acting in his own name, or as the instrument of God's mercies, he will only use those powers on special occasions, and for special purposes. He will not, at his temptation, turn the stones into bread; he will wait till he can get food in the ordinary way. He will ask the Samaritan woman to draw water for him. He will cross the Sea of Galilee, ordinarily, on ship-board, though we know that he could walk on the water if he liked. The reason of that, I suppose, is that he wanted to be indebted to his creatures. As a child, he would be suckled at his Mother's breast, dying, he would accept a draught of wine from his executioner. From that, too, we have something to learn; we have to learn to accept kindness and help from one another, not to refuse it, as we so often do, out of pride. The disciple is not above his Master; if he was not ashamed to be indebted to his fellow-men, how should we?

So much for the powers of the Incarnate; now for his knowledge; how much did he know, as Man? The theologians teach that he enjoyed, as Man, the beatific vision which is granted to the saints in heaven, since this is evidently not beyond the compass of a perfect humanity. He was *simul comprehensor et viator*. I haven't time to go into it; but if you think for a moment of the Gospel record, you'll be struck by the way in which he is always represented as having strange insight into what was happening at the moment, clear prevision of what was to happen in the future. Constantly he reads the thought in other people's minds. He prophesies, not once but several times over, the fact of his Passion and the manner of it; his betrayal, his desertion by the apostles, his Resurrection. And when he does ask a question, I think you can say that it is nearly always the sort of question a teacher asks, not because he wants to know but because he wants to draw the other person out. "Whose image is there on this coin?" "What did Moses command you?" "Who do men say that I am?"—as if he had no way of finding out things like that for himself!

But, of course, all that creates a difficulty. If he knew so much that is hidden from the ordinary human being, in the present or in the past, how could he have a real human experience? And how can it be true to say that he increased in wisdom and knowledge? It is easy to possess *powers* without using them; can one possess knowledge, and not use it? Well, it is universally agreed that our Lord did have experimental knowledge as well; he did *learn* things. How he combined these two different avenues of experience, I don't think we can really guess. It's a mystery to us, because we have never had the beatific vision. But it might look quite simple, if we knew more about the beatific vision. If you possessed, at this moment, all the knowledge which it is possible for man to have, it would not all be equally present to your mind at this moment. Some act of attention, of focusing, would be necessary before you got at the piece of knowledge you wanted, at any given time, to use. So it may be that there is not really so much difficulty as we think about the idea of our Lord at Nazareth learning things which he knew already, if they were somehow in the background of his mind when he learnt them.

At the same time, we have to recognize that our Lord's privileged position in this respect made him different from us others. He could not, if you come to think of it, exercise the virtue of faith, strictly so called, because faith must have a dim, not a clear view of its object; nor the virtue of hope, strictly so called, because hope implies an uncertainty about the future. But he could—such a strange thing is our human fashioning—experience on the Cross such an obscuration of his powers as made him *feel* as if God had deserted him. That is difficult, if you like, to understand, but I don't think we ought to find it difficult to accept, because it is vouched for by the people who ought to know, as far as anybody can know, what such dereliction means—the saints who have written on mystical theology. He could not doubt; he could not despair; but he reached, I suppose, if we may dare to speculate on such a subject, that borderline of spiritual darkness in which the reason itself, with whatever of certitude it possesses, becomes like a beleaguered citadel with the enemy battering at its gates.

And that brings me on to the last part of our subject. God is all-holy; and it is evident that Christ as Man reflected that holiness in a unique degree. Only, are we to think of that holiness in him as a peaceful, undisturbed possession which could feel no shock of assault from without? Or are we to think of it as maintained by an effort, in the face of difficulties? What freedom of choice did our Lord enjoy? Would it have been possible for him to commit sin?

The answer to that question is a very simple one. Catholic theology teaches that our Lord possessed a privilege even higher than the privilege granted to our Lady. The privilege conferred on her by her immaculate Conception was that of *posse non peccare*, being able not to sin; the curse of Eden was revoked in her. But our Lord as Man had the still higher privilege of *non posse peccare*, not being able to sin. We catch our breath for a moment when the archangel comes to our Lady and tells her of her sublime destiny; it was within her power to say "No." But when our Lord is tempted in the wilderness, as we shall read in next Sunday's gospel, it was impossible that he should yield; we can have no doubt, no abstract doubt even, of the issue. Why then, you ask, what was the point of the temptation? And is our Lord's temptation really a very useful model for us, when it was no real test, only a kind of demonstration?

Well, I don't want to steal next Sunday's gospel from next Sunday's preacher. I'll only say this, that the temptation in the wilderness is the story of an effort by the devil to find out whether our Lord was just man or something more than man; it was a true test in that sense, although the devil got nothing out of it. Our Lord, it must be admitted, did not share the moral struggles we go through, because we have a traitor within the citadel, our own corrupt nature; he could only know temptation as something external to himself. But that does not mean his example is no use to us as a model. Sinless, he fought sin with those same weapons which he wanted us sinners to use; self-denial, prudence, and humility.

I have been spending all my time, I am afraid, in pointing out to you what our Lord's Incarnation doesn't mean. Let me remind you, in conclusion, of what it does mean. It means that God made Man has experienced cold, hunger, thirst, fatigue, sleeplessness, bodily suffering of the most intense kind; that he has known the emotions of love, pity, indignation, joy, grief, and bodily fear; that he has suffered from the neighbourhood of evil, and of the Prince of evil himself; that he has allowed himself to descend into the depths of spiritual desolation; that he has worked, and watched, and prayed, and lived the life of common men, and accepted benefits from them, and consolation in sadness. It is such a Master we serve; one who shares with us the experience of everything in our nature, except what is degrading to it, of every accident in our fortunes except what results, immediately, from sin. In the bond of that common experience he offers us a human friendship; a friendship which survives neglect and coldness on our part, which follows every movement of ours with anxious solicitude, and does not end with death.

XVIII

IMMORTALITY

IT is a thing we should always be careful about when we enter into any discussion, especially with non-Catholics, about our religious beliefs, to distinguish between the knowledge which mere reason would give us, even apart from revelation, and the knowledge about which we should have no certainty at all if it had not been revealed to us. That the soul is immortal is demonstrable by philosophy; you can see that from the existence of pagan treatises on the subject, like the *Phædo* of Plato. That is not to say that it is a necessary part of every Catholic's beliefs to be able to prove it or even to follow the proofs of it. They do not make themselves evident to all minds; and some minds are less ready than others to enter into metaphysical considerations. You are perfectly within your rights, therefore, if you say, "Personally I can't keep up with all this abstruse reasoning, and I believe that my soul is immortal because the Church, depending upon a revelation from God himself, tells me that it is." But at the same time you ought to know that there is a philosophical method of argument by which this truth can be established; otherwise it will bother you to feel that many of your non-Catholic friends, who do not admit the claims of revelation, have no means of reaching a certainty which is, obviously, of such importance for the regulation of our everyday lives.

But when we get beyond that, when we discuss doctrines

like those of heaven, hell, and purgatory, then we *have* to take revelation for our guide, because our human reason does not enable us to reach any certainty here. We could make guesses, of course; these notions are not merely Christian notions, and you will find them worked out with great elaborateness by some of the heathen writers; in Plato's *Republic*, for example, or in the sixth book of the *Æneid*; and the necessity of a system of rewards and punishments beyond the grave seemed evident to so critical a mind as that of Immanuel Kant. But we should only be guessing, really, if revealed theology did not come to our aid. Now, what I want to do this morning is to bridge the gap a little between immortality as it is viewed from the standpoint of natural theology, and what the Church tells us about a future life. Do we know anything—this is what I want to ask—about what our immortality is or is not *like*, by our natural reason? Or do we merely know that immortality is a fact, without understanding anything about its nature? For we shall hear our non-Catholic friends discussing immortality, and we shall hear them arriving at all sorts of strange conclusions; can we tell them anything about the conclusions which they ought to arrive at?

First let us notice this; that immortality, even philosophically considered, necessarily means *personal* immortality. You will sometimes find people nowadays who accept, quite cheerfully and with conviction, the idea that life survives beyond the grave, and yet, when you question them, will take the gilt off the gingerbread entirely by explaining that they do not mean personal immortality after all. The soul is not snuffed out like a candle at death, no; but it is absorbed, they will tell you, into a kind of reservoir of spirit, like a drop falling into the ocean. If you are religiously minded, you will say that the soul after death becomes absorbed in God; if you are not religiously minded, you will say that it becomes absorbed in a universal principle of life, whatever that may mean; but in either case its conscious identity will perish; there will no longer be a *you*, remembering its own past, enjoying its own present experience, looking forward to the personal experience of an endless future. Death will not be annihilation, but it will be, if we may use a quite vulgar illustration, something like getting lost in the wash.

I think the reason why men's minds fall easily into such a mistake is very largely this—that in all languages the soul, or the spirit, is apt to be described by a word borrowed from our material experience which means *breath*, just that and nothing more. You see, as there is nothing else like the soul in our experience, nothing that we can possibly compare it with, men were driven to describe it by a metaphor, and an obviously inadequate metaphor. There is no reason in the world why we should go about thinking of the soul as if it were a kind of gas. Such a description gives us some faint idea of its immateriality; but no kind of clue as to its inner nature. And I suggest that these people who talk as if the soul would be absorbed after death are only, after all, going one better than people like Sir Arthur Keith, who tells us that it will be snuffed out like a candle. According to these people, it will not be snuffed out like a candle, but will be turned off like a jet of gas. They think of the human race as a vast collection of gas-jets, which burn all right for a time until they run into a motor-bus or something, and then are immediately turned off. Well, of course, that does not mean annihilation. The gas still exists when the tap is turned off, but it exists only as part of a huge volume of gas, the greater part of which is stored up in those enormous gasometers by the Ferry Hinksey backwater. So the soul, they think, when it leaves the body is just a kind of vapour, which forms part of a huge volume of vapour that is floating about somewhere, we don't quite know where.

Now, all that is assuming that what we know about the

soul is derived from what we know about our fellow-men. What we know about our fellow-man is that just before the moment we call death he is capable of self-determined movement, or apparently self-determined movement, whereas after the moment which we call death he is just a lump of matter which lies there inert. What is it that has gone out of him? Nothing that we know of by our experience; nothing, for all we can tell, more than what has gone out of a fly when we crush it on the window-pane. But, if you come to think of it, what we know about the soul is not derived from what we observe in our fellow-men; from what they look like, whether before or after death, or from the way in which they behave during life. Our experience of the soul comes from inside; you are conscious, directly conscious, of your own soul, not of anybody else's. When you think, you are conscious of yourself as thinking; you can become the object of your own thought. And it is true to say that that soul of yours is half of your experience. All your experiences can be divided into two; the thing which you experience, and yourself as experiencing it. That soul of yours is something known directly; so that there is much more to be said for the subjective idealist, who refuses to believe that anything exists except his own soul, than for the materialist, who doubts the existence of the soul altogether.

The soul, then, as it is given us in this lonely, individual experience of conscious life—what do we know about what it is like? We know it as something individual, which does not mix with anything else, which can hold no commerce with anything else except through the medium of the body. How extraordinary it is, when you come to think of it, that I, when I want to put my ideas before your minds, should have to instruct all sorts of little cells in my brain to set all sorts of little muscles going in my tongue and lips, these movements setting up a series of vibrations in the air, which act upon

6*

certain nerves in the drums of your ears, and so, by way of
the material brain, can convey impressions to your immortal
mind! But this is what is happening now; there is no short
cut to be reached between one soul and another. The soul,
then, is given to us in experience as a lonely, individual thing;
it is also given to us in experience as an indivisible thing. You
can't imagine your soul being cut in half. You talk of it as
being divided up into intellect, will and memory; but it isn't
really divided. Your will is you, the whole of you, willing;
your intellect is you, the whole of you, thinking. There is no
such thing as half your soul. And if the soul is thus individual
and indivisible, it isn't like a gas-jet at all. If you cannot
imagine it as cut in half, equally you cannot think of two souls
as somehow merged into one. If each soul is a lonely point of
experience, you cannot imagine a whole multitude of souls
losing each its own consciousness and absorbed into a kind of
world-consciousness instead. This whole doctrine of souls
after death getting lost in the wash is false to everything we
know about the soul in our human experience.

Well, I mustn't delay longer over that; I must pass on to
another doctrine which you will sometimes find defended by
the extraordinary loose thinking of our day. Not that it is a
new doctrine at all; it is an extremely old doctrine, to which
the human mind is apt to return when religious certainties
grow weak. I mean the doctrine of metempsychosis, or the
transmigration of souls. You have all come across that theory
at school, when you read the classics; the great exponent of it,
as you will remember, was Pythagoras, the philosopher who
found a shield hung up in a temple, which was reputed to
have belonged to Euphorbus, a warrior killed in the Trojan
war, and proceeded to claim the shield as his own because, as
he said, it had just occurred to him that he had been Euphorbus in a previous life. It would certainly be a very comfortable
doctrine for anybody who is fond of picking up antiques. His

thought had a profound influence on the speculations of antiquity, and you will find traces of it both in Plato and in Virgil. And remember, the idea of reincarnation has this attraction for the human mind, that it suggests a convenient way in which the wrongs and unhappinesses of this world can be redressed. Who knows if your fate in a future incarnation may not be determined by the way in which you behave in this present incarnation of yours? So that one soul can go on passing from one life into another, now happy now unhappy according as it has met or failed to meet its earlier opportunities, and that process continues *ad infinitum*?

I don't know whether it is fanciful to suggest that ideas of that sort are again encouraged, in these modern days, by an inadequate metaphor taken from contemporary science, taken this time not from gas but from electricity. After all, a single unit of electricity may express itself in various different ways, either pushing along the train you are sitting in, or lighting up your room, or producing a nasty, inhuman sort of heat in one of those electric stoves they give you nowadays instead of fires. Why should not the soul be something like an electric spark, which finds expression now in this way, now in that; at one time as a human being, let us say, and at another time as a cow or a tadpole? I don't know that there is any body of responsible people who seriously assert that this is so, except perhaps the theosophists. But you will find people speculating whether it might not be so, and refusing to accept the Christian idea of eternity in consequence. Now, what are we going to say to that kind of person?

I don't think you can say with truth that, in the light of mere reason, such speculations are absolutely impossible. You can say everything short of that; you can say that they rest on no shadow of proof, and moreover that they are extraordinarily improbable, because they are quite out of line with what we do know about the soul. If, of course, people who believed in them believed in them as part of a revelation, and were prepared to give us credentials by which the truth of that revelation could be recognized, we should stop to consider them. But no such credentials are forthcoming; nor is there any proof of these assertions in themselves. Of course, people will quote you Wordsworth's ode on the intimations of immortality and tell you that you do now and again have that odd experience of remembering something which, you are sure, never happened in this life; finding a landscape or a scene familiar, for example, although you are quite certain that you were never there before. But all that, you see, whatever be the explanation of it, is really the exception which proves the rule. If their doctrine were true, we ought to be remembering things all the time. Or at least we ought to carry away considerable memories of a past life, instead of these vague flashes which a psychologist will explain to you in any number of different ways.

But, worse than being unproved, that doctrine is, as I say, out of line with all we do know about the soul. You see, one of the characteristic activities of the human soul is memory. It is true that memory can be interrupted by physical influences, a fall off a horse, for example, which may make a person forget a whole lot of things which have gone before it. But such a loss of memory is never total; even if you forget your own name you will remember that two and two make four. And if, for example, you challenge me to prove that I am the same person who was a fellow of Trinity in 1914, I do so by appealing to the phenomenon of continuous memory. Or if you challenge me, rather more fantastically, to prove that you are not me, I shall say, "Tell me what intention I said Mass for yesterday, and if you can remember that, then I shall begin to consider the question whether you are me." Now, this phenomenon of memory, linking up all our experiences and dividing so sharply the total of my experience from the total of yours, has disappeared, it seems, when you and I find ourselves reincarnated in a different life. What confidence, then, are we to feel that some soul a hundred years hence will be identical with yours or mine, when the very hall-mark of conscious identity, namely memory, is absent from it?

You can say, then, that these speculations are very improbable. But it is only when you take revelation into account that you can be absolutely certain they are wrong. *It remains to men once to die, and after that the judgment*; that is the faith of the Christian Church. And that faith has practical consequences, of terrible importance. Your personality will not become lost and merged after death; it will live on, with all the liabilities it contracted here. And on the other side it will not be living a second human life like this, in which it will be able to retrieve past mistakes and atone for past errors. This life is the *one* chance given us of proving whether we want to be found friends of God or not; no argument of human philosophy encourages us to think otherwise, and divine revelation assures us that it is so.

There is one other point I would like to touch on, in which Catholic theology differs from many loose speculations of to-day. And here we have only revelation to guide us; human reasoning could have given us no light on the subject at all. The point I mean is this; that the attitude of the soul at the moment of death has a decisive importance for eternity. If you get into an argument about this, you will almost certainly find that your non-Catholic friend has different ideas about it; he thinks, you will find, that after you are dead Almighty God simply adds up in one list all the sins you have committed, and in another list all the good actions you have done, strikes a kind of balance between the two, and pronounces sentence accordingly. Now, I don't say that there is no truth at all in such a notion; I don't say it is probable, for example, that God would allow a soul which has been really trying faithfully to serve him for years upon years to fall away from him at the very last. But we do know that a soul can be saved by grace at the last moment of a mis-spent life; that is certain in the case of the Penitent Thief; and we may hope, please God, that it has been true in countless other lives, even where there was no external sign given of a death-bed contrition. Which clearly means that the moment of death is, as I say, a moment of decisive importance; and that you and I ought to pray for perseverance, and for the grace of a Christian death, even when the event seems remote and our spiritual state gives us no special cause for anxiety. Life doesn't just depend upon being good and being bad; God's grace is what we want to pray for, and pray for all the more earnestly in proportion as we are humble enough to realize that we cannot do without it.

XIX

THE CHURCH AND HUMAN PROGRESS

THE two parables of the Mustard Seed and the Leaven are a pair, and are obviously meant to be a pair. Our Lord seems to have been fond of this method; partly, I suppose, on the principle that if you give two illustrations of a moral which you want to rub in, you can make sure of people seeing the real point, instead of going off on side issues; any speaker will tell you that. Partly, perhaps, because his audiences were mixed, and an illustration which would appeal to one set of them would not appeal to others. There were men there and women; and so you find him asking, "What *man* is there among you that hath a hundred sheep, and if he lose one of them . . ." and then, "Or what *woman* is there having ten groats, if she lose one of them . . ."—he will suit his lesson to both classes. And so here; the kingdom of heaven is like a mustard seed which *a man* took and planted in his field; or again it is like to leaven which *a woman* took and hid in three measures of meal. It is part of our Lord's great courtesy, that he will make allowances for everyone.

But at the same time you will find this about the parables which our Lord gives us in pairs; that the moral is not always quite the same in either case; the second will give it a slightly different twist from the first. And so it is here. By the kingdom of heaven our Lord customarily means, as I hope we all know, not the future life which we shall enjoy in heaven, but his Church on earth, which is the appointed means of conducting us to it. If there was nothing else to assure us of that, these two parables would be sufficient proof of it. Our Lord did not occupy his whole time, while he preached on earth, in expounding a philosophy of unworldliness, of sincerity, of forbearance, of loving our enemies, and so on. He came to found a Church; and he foresaw how that Church would develop through the centuries, and has prophesied for us, though it be only in rough outline, its development. And in these two parables, evidently, he is telling us how his Church is destined to grow. How small it looked, when he stood there and preached to groups of peasants standing by the lake of Galilee; or when, after his Ascension, a hundred and twenty souls waited in the upper room for the coming of the Holy Spirit—just so the mustard seed is small; just so the bit of leaven is insignificant in size compared with the three measures of meal which are to be leavened by it. The influence of the Church grew secretly; people who lived in those early centuries didn't know what was happening, until they suddenly found that communities of Christians had sprung up in every corner of the empire; so the growth of a tree, or the working of leaven, is something hidden from us; we cannot stand by and watch it happening. The extension of his Church was an irresistible force; just so, given proper conditions of soil, the seed must develop; just so the leaven inevitably corrupts the unleavened meal with which it comes in contact. In all that, you see, the two parables are alike.

But there are other aspects, and very important aspects in which they differ. And in this above all; that the growth of the mustard seed shows you the Christian Church as a body which swells in size, whereas the spread of the leaven shows you the Christian gospel as an influence which radiates force and communicates it to its neighbourhood. The tree *takes* something *from* its surroundings; takes nourishment from the earth and the moisture and the sunlight, and so grows bigger: and the Church takes something from her surroundings, takes the souls of men from the world and incorporates them into herself. The leaven *gives* something *to* its surroundings, infects them with its own life; so the Christian gospel gives something to its surroundings; communicates to mankind its own spirit of discipline and its own philosophy of life. Both those processes, then, we should expect to see at work when we watch the development of the Christian Church in history.

And so far as the first part of the parable is concerned, the lesson of the mustard tree, there is no great difficulty in recognizing the description. Of course, it is quite true that the growth of the Church in mere numbers is not a steady, uniform process; it is chequered, again and again, by schisms and heresies from within, by persecutions from without, by world developments generally. But, in a sense, that makes it all the more remarkable; mere uninterrupted growth would not be so strong a proof of life beating within as the power to recover from a series of shocks and mutilations. This miracle of the Church's continual reviviscence is recognized even by outside, even by unfriendly critics. You probably know Macaulay's almost despairing passage in the essay on von Ranke, when he is writing about the state of Europe after the French Revolution: "The Arabs have a fable that the Great Pyramid was built by antediluvian kings, and alone of all the works of men bore the weight of the flood. Such as this was the fate of the Papacy. It had been buried under the great inundation; but its deep foundations had remained unshaken, and when the waters abated, it appeared alone amidst the ruins of a world which had passed away." That was written a hundred years ago; but the testimony is true of our own period. You have only to read history to realize that the mustard seed has grown.

But the leaven—has the leaven worked? There you will not find the critics of our religion forced into such attitudes of unwilling admission. I think the criticism which we find it most uncomfortable to meet is when they tell us that the Catholic Church is all right when you consider it *a priori*, on paper, as a system, but when you look at its actual record in history you do not find its effects on human life the kind of effects which you would expect a supernatural institution to have. The world, to be sure, has advanced a great deal since the times of our Lord. Slavery has given place to freedom, savagery to kindness, selfishness to philanthropy; men are no longer (in the more favoured countries) executed for slight offences, or tortured when they refuse to give evidence, or killed in duels; some attempt is made, at any rate, to give working men decent wages, and rescue them and their families from destitution; and in a thousand other ways it is possible to show that the world has become a more comfortable place to live in. But how much, we are asked, has all this to do with Christianity, or at any rate with the Catholic Church? Is it not true that the improvements which have been made in the condition of human living have been made, for the most part, without any effort of sympathy on the part of Catholics, and sometimes in the teeth of their opposition? And if that is so, how can we claim that the Catholic Church, as we find the Catholic Church in history, is the Church which our Lord referred to in his parables? How strange that the leaven which has leavened the world has not, noticeably at any rate, proceeded from her!

The answer to that kind of objection is not an easy one, and I think it is rather a humiliating one. Perhaps the simplest way to put it is this. During the period between the Ascension and the Reformation, that charge is not true. During the period between the Reformation and the French Revolution that charge is true, but it was not our fault; in great measure at least it was not our fault. In our own day, the situation has grown so desperately complicated that it defies analysis. What seems to emerge from it is that under modern conditions we Catholics ought, more than ever, to be taking the lead in enlightening the conscience of the world; that, largely, we are not doing it, and it is our fault that we are not doing it; and moreover, that in proportion as we do succeed in our efforts, we shall not be given any credit for it; we shall be cried down as much as ever by the prophets of materialistic humanitarianism for not going about it in a different and more wholehearted way.

It is quite true that the Catholic Church has never made social reform the first plank in her programme; you might say that where she leavens society she always does so in a fit of absence of mind. Her message has always been addressed to the individual soul, rather than to the political community. St Paul could tell masters to be kind to their slaves, without saying they must set them free; and it was only gradually that slavery itself, or even the cruel sports of the amphitheatre, were abolished. It was only gradually that serfdom disappeared in the Middle Ages. But these changes did happen, and in the meantime the world had learned more respect for women, more sympathy for the poor; education became more general, laws became less harsh in their enforcement, as the spirit of the Christian religion asserted itself. You cannot pick out the names of the great reformers, but that was because the whole process was so gradual and almost unconscious; gradual, yes, and unnoticed, but that is the way of the leaven when it goes to work.

Since the Reformation, or perhaps you ought to say since the great schism which divided the world shortly before the Reformation, it has been true on the whole that the Church was no longer responsible for civilizing the world; but then, it was not altogether her fault. The Protestants, in the first days of the Reformation, were not a yard ahead of her; and as late as the middle of the eighteenth century you could find a man like Whitefield, the great Methodist preacher, owning slaves. But the point is that the Church was on the defensive, almost everywhere; she had to consolidate her own position against rival claimants; and she exhausted much of her strength and of her sanctity in propaganda or in controversy. Nor were the Popes able, in those days of stress and contention, to impose their will on Catholic nations. The worst evils of slavery flourished, in spite of energetic protests; duelling was maintained by the social fashion of an age, in spite of stringent condemnations of it. Again, it is to be remembered that the most prominent Catholic nation during most of that period was France; and France was sitting very loose to its ecclesiastical obedience; the Pope's word did not run among the French clergy as it runs nowadays. Catholics were too much concerned over the future of the mustard seed to notice much what was happening to the leaven.

With the French Revolution, a new phase sets in. In England and in the United States you could hardly expect Catholics to take any prominent share in the business of reform, because their numbers were infinitesimal. In the various European countries where the Church was still strong, she found herself everywhere attacked by the same people who were using the language of humanitarianism and of reform. Men were slow to distinguish her, and perhaps it must be admitted that she was slow to distinguish herself, from those parties of mere reaction which the new Liberalism assailed. And that difficulty persists right down to our own day. Only, of course, in our day the issues are not so direct as they seemed in the last century. The cry for reform has given place to a cry for revolution; the language of hate has replaced, among the humanitarians, the language of love. And all over Europe new nationalisms have grown up, sometimes friendly to the Church, sometimes at issue with her, but always in their inspiration something foreign to her thought. Meanwhile, both in our own country and still more across the Atlantic, Catholic numbers have grown, especially among the more educated classes, and the influences of the other Christianities has waned, so that men look to the Church, more than they did formerly, to tell them what the Christian religion really preaches. That means that we have a greater responsibility than our parents and our grandparents had for diffusing, in a world that has begun to take notice of us, the leaven of Christian charity.

Only, don't think that we are going to get any credit for it. Don't imagine I am suggesting that we Catholics ought to take a greater share than we do in the fight for human happiness because it will be good propaganda for our religion if we do. For the whole of your lifetimes, probably, everything that we Catholics do or propose to do in that line will be viewed with suspicion, will be misrepresented; we shall be told that we are only half-hearted reformers, trying to take the wind out of other people's sails. That is because we cannot afford to neglect principles, cannot afford to leave out one half of the truth. We have got to love peace, without despising and belittling man's instinct of patriotism; we have got to redress injustice without violating essential human liberties; we have got to work for the relief of human misery without defying the sanctities of the divine law. So we shall always be at a disadvantage compared with other reformers who can only see one set of principles at a time, and we shall get no thanks for our interference.

Why is it, then, that we have got to take our part, more than we did, in trying to make this temporary world of ours a better place to live in? Because the Gospel of Christ is essentially a leaven, a dynamic force in human affairs, and we shall be false to our whole vocation if we treat the imperfections of human society as if they were something that didn't matter. We shall be tempted to do so; we are tempted to do so. The world around us is so full of social experiments and of party war-cries, and the people who are keen on these things are generally such boring people to meet, that we are tempted to throw ourselves back on our isolation and say, "Well, there's no room in the world for any more reformers just now; as long as I live a decent Catholic life in private, I can afford to spend my time dancing and going to the pictures and getting all the fun out of life that I can." To do that is to starve the instincts of your age and period, a dangerous thing to do. Don't, for heaven's sake, imagine that I am recommending you all to spend your time up here going to meetings, signing petitions and carrying them round for other people to sign, and contributing to the kind of book or magazine which is understood to be the finest flower of recent undergraduate thought. It is quite extraordinary what a lot of good is not done by that sort of thing. No, what I am suggesting is that, since you are here to be educated, you should pay some attention—whatever attention your ordinary work and engagements permit—to getting some grasp of the problems which are exercising the modern world; and not merely studying these in the light of your religion, so that you may be able to give a good account of what the Church teaches, and why, and why on certain subjects she has no special teaching to offer, although everybody else in the world has a ready-made solution of his own. I am suggesting that you should prepare yourselves here for taking a decent amount of interest in public affairs later on, and making your own contribution to the needs of your time, according to your opportunities.

One word needs to be added, not less important. Our Lord says that the mustard tree is to grow out of all recognition;

he doesn't say that it is to grow indefinitely; does not mean us to understand that there will ever be a time at which the whole of mankind will be even nominally Christian. His prophecy that his Gospel will be preached in the whole world is sufficiently fulfilled if all mankind has a real chance of hearing it. Similarly, when he says that the leaven hidden in the meal spread till the whole was leavened, I don't think we are necessarily to understand this as meaning that there will be a time at which the principles of Christian charity towards one's neighbour will dominate the counsels of humanity. We are to understand that the Christian message will make itself felt throughout the world which harbours it, not necessarily that it will triumph. Don't be disappointed, therefore, if it appears —it may perfectly well come to appear so in your lifetime—as if things were going backwards instead of forwards, as if the world were relapsing into barbarism instead of following along the path marked out for it by what we call civilization. Don't be disappointed, above all, if during your lifetime the Church, despite her best efforts, still seems to be fighting a rearguard action, and losing, if anything, in the modern struggle for existence. As I said before, the social influence of the Church is in reality a by-product of her activity; it is not her life. Her business, ultimately, is with the individual soul, and the promises by which she lives are not limited within these narrow horizons. The leaven is there, and it does not lose its virtue with the centuries. But whether in our particular age the time is ripe for its manifestation, that we cannot know. God's view is longer than ours, and for all we can tell we may be living in the early Church still; our modern troubles may be only the growing-pains of Christianity. It will be our fault if we lose heart.

XX

THE THREE MORALITIES

WANT to give you a sort of sketch of the history of Christian morals, with special reference to the cleavage between the Catholic and the Protestant notions of morality since the Reformation, and the consequences of that cleavage in the thought of our own day. It is an extremely elaborate subject, about which I am always hoping to write an enormous book in two volumes, but I don't see when I am going to get the time. This sketch, therefore, will be very sketchy indeed.

I think the thing that puzzles us about Christian morals, if you come to think of it, is the question: Does the Church keep two codes of morals, one for the saint and one for the sinner? One code which is meant for those who aspire to perfection, represented by the teaching of the Sermon on the Mount; and another for ordinary people, represented by the moral theology books which are always defining the exact conditions of a mortal sin, and almost encouraging us—we sometimes feel—to commit venial sins by showing us what a lot of sinful actions there are which nevertheless do not cut us off from sanctifying grace? And if there are really two codes, what is the relation between them? Well, the history of Christian morals is very largely concerned with that point. It is very largely the history of a refusal, on the part of the Catholic Church, to draw the minimum line of Christian

174

conduct too high; so high that in our imperfect world a great number of souls would be unable to live up to it, or even to see any hope of living up to it, and therefore would drop away from the practice of religion in despair. Whereas the heretics in all ages, the Montanists in the first age of the Church, the Jansenists in days whose influence has scarcely died out even now, were always for tightening things up; for binding Christians, as if under pain of mortal sin, to a rule of perfection, very admirable in itself and very desirable if you could enforce it, but not meant, so it seems, for our imperfect world. As Mr Arnold Lunn put it, in a correspondence which he and I published, "The Catholic Church realizes that she cannot afford to be too exclusive. In the course of nineteen centuries she has at least made one great discovery; she has learned that sinners sometimes sin. And as a result Catholicism is more successful than Protestantism in retaining the affectionate loyalty of the erring."

I don't think there can be much doubt that the very early Church had stricter views on moral subjects than we have. There are many reasons for that. All the early Christians were converts, and in the first fervours of their conversion they meant business. Many of them, probably, imagined that it could not be long now before our Lord returned to earth for the final judgment; they lived with the feeling that the sky might at any moment crack above their heads. The fact of becoming Christians marked them off sharply from the pagan world which surrounded them; and the daily spectacle of heathen immoralities drove them, by reaction, into a fervour of revolt. Before long, too, persecution began; and that meant that the Church was purged of her weaker members and only attracted those souls who were prepared to make heroic efforts in order to achieve salvation. Accordingly, you will find the early Fathers condemning, wholesale, various kinds of dissipation which nowadays we should only consider wrong for some people or in some circumstances—the theatre, for example, or dancing; you will find that the ideal of virginity is preached with a wealth of rhetorical expression which makes the unsympathetic modern reader imagine that Christians think of marriage as something wicked; you will find terrifically heavy penances imposed, according to our modern ideas, for various offences, especially for giving way under persecution and going through the formality of offering incense to the heathen gods. Yes, we sometimes feel that the early Church wouldn't have been quite the place for you and me; but even in the early Church you find exaggerations of that tendency; you find a rigorism which the Church has to disown, at the risk of making those who are its preachers fall away into heresy.

The Montanists were the first; they are an extraordinarily interesting set of people, and bear a strong resemblance to some of the Puritan sects which arose in later days. You cannot read far in the writings of Tertullian, their great champion, without coming across the most exaggerated descriptions of the world's wickedness and the holiness which is demanded of all Christians. One particular notion of theirs, which serves to illustrate their point of view, is that a widow who married again was committing mortal sin. The early Church didn't encourage second marriages very much; you will see in the New Testament that the "widows" formed a separate and honoured body among the congregation; a very formidable body, one would think. But it wasn't enough for the Montanists to exalt widowhood as a kind of state of perfection; they would have it that remarriage was actually wrong. Then there were the Novatians, who held that a man who had once lapsed in time of persecution could never be restored to Communion, even at the moment of death; and there were the Donatists, who held that bishops and priests who had given up copies of the sacred books to heathen pursuivants lost, *ipso facto*, the validity of their ordination. In these cases, the Church let herself in for the competition of powerful schisms, which lasted for centuries, rather than fall in with their over-strict ideas; rather than admit that genuine contrition can be unavailing, or that the validity of a priest's acts can depend on the holiness of his life. It wasn't that the Church, in the main, disapproved of the ideals preached by these heretics, but she wouldn't have those ideals forced down everybody's throat as a condition of being a member of the Christian Church at all.

Chesterton in his book on St Francis has a very interesting chapter, in which he works out the idea that the Church during the later empire and the dark ages was going through a period of expiation, of atonement, for the sins of the pagan world which went before it. The Christian message had to be something that seems to us severe, that seems to us gloomy, because the world, then, was painfully purging out of its system the poisons of pagan degeneracy. It was in the twelfth century, he says, that Christians began to be able to look on the natural beauty of the world and enjoy all God's gifts in the natural creation without feeling that there was something corrupt, something defiling about them.

In the early Middle Ages you see, for a moment, the natural instincts of man and his supernatural hope reduced to a harmony; you see it in all the pageantry and the fun and the chivalry and the revival of art which, in spite of all the wars and all the horrors, mark out that period of human history in gold. Then corruption set in again; and as a protest against that corruption you get movements like those of the Waldenses and the Poor Men of Lyons, criticizing the worldliness of priests and of bishops, and the luxuries of the times in general; you get Wyclif and the Lollards threatening the fabric of society by claiming that a landlord has no title to his possessions unless he is a good Christian. Once again, you see, the reaction against worldliness, a reaction perfectly justified in itself, takes heretical form by wanting to go too far. And so it leads up to the Reformation. We shall deceive ourselves if we think of the Reformation as merely a matter of doctrinal differences, or merely a conflict between the new nobilities and the old tradition of Europe. In part, at least, the Reformation was a genuine protest against the corrupt state of morals which followed on the Renaissance. And where the Reformers got the upper hand, uncontrolled by secular princes, they overdid their part by trying to introduce a discipline far stricter than the discipline of the Catholic Church had been before them. In Scotland, for example, a person guilty of adultery who refused to submit to the discipline of the Kirk was put under the greater excommunication, solemnly given over into the power and hands of the devil, and outlawed from Christian society. If the Reformation had really succeeded, the sinners of Europe would have lived under conditions of intolerable oppression.

The Reformation did not succeed; kings and courts were too strong for it, and it made terms with the world after all. But it left its mark on society by creating, among certain classes, a tradition of Puritanism which has not yet died out. In England and Scotland, at any rate, a system of rigorism in morals commended itself to, and imbedded itself in, the mentality of the lower middle class. I am not saying that contemptuously, though you will often find such terms used in contempt. A class that has to be frugal, has to maintain a certain standard of respectability, that is excluded from the freer activities of the landed gentry, easily develops and clings to a tradition of Puritanism. There is no room for it in the theatre; it is too poor for the dress circle, too refined for the pit. It has no money to waste on racing or on gambling; it is too superior to join in the rough dances of the countryside, too provincial to acquire the manners of the ballroom.

Finally, in England, though not in Scotland, it loses the tradition of drinking intoxicants, because it is too proud for the public houses and cannot afford to belong to clubs; so a temperance movement rounds off the completeness of the Puritan mentality. That mentality ruled England yesterday, and is making a hard struggle against defeat at this moment. It still wants to enforce a stricter morality by law, in the same spirit in which Calvin and John Knox made the attempt three and a half centuries ago.

In Catholic countries, and in a Catholic society which manages to maintain itself, as ours did for more than two centuries, quite outside the general life of the nation, this Puritan ideal has never ruled. You get approaches to it; the tendency in our own Church is labelled, rather loosely, by the seventeenth-century nickname of Jansenism. The Curé d'Ars at the beginning of last century was not satisfied until he had banished dancing altogether from his parish; and even to-day, where the influence of the priesthood is strong, as in Ireland or in French Canada, you will find it exercised, sometimes, in a rather rigorist spirit. But it is an influence that remains personal; a Catholic society, however strict in its views, has no itch for moral legislation, such as Puritanism has. It will only frame laws for the repression of vice where it is necessary to preserve the whole structure of social life, as, for example, in the matter of legalized divorce.

Now, when a society goes pagan, as our society is going pagan hand over hand—that is not pulpit rhetoric, it is plain fact for anybody who takes the trouble to think—you get three distinct reactions on the part of Christian thought. There is the Puritan reaction; the reaction of the ordinary Protestant mind which has never been captured by Puritanism; and the reaction of the Catholic minority. The public effort of Puritanism is a wild attempt to resist all the proposals it dislikes, without distinguishing between them; no sweepstakes, no Sunday cinemas, no penny off beer, no, no, no. And where you have a revival of religion among non-Catholics it will fall, automatically, into the Puritan way of thinking, because that has become traditional with us; so that your Buchmanite, if one may judge by the scraps of information one gets about that movement, will tend even to think of smoking as something inconsistent with the Christian life, instead of an indulgence which, like other indulgences, may laudably be given up by a person aiming at perfection.

On the other hand, the non-Puritan Protestant public finds itself completely at sea; it does not know what attitude to adopt towards the paganizing of life. You see, for years, and you may almost say for centuries, the only reason the ordinary Englishman has known for not doing a thing was because it was something that was not done. But when something that was not done suddenly turns into something that is done, all his standards are upset. To take a very small and not an important instance of what I mean, women making up their faces was, thirty years ago, among the things that were not done; not officially, anyhow, not in public. And, of course, that applies to more serious things; it applies, for example, to divorce. Your ordinary Englishman is absolutely bewildered on that point. He knows that divorce was not done thirty years ago, and that it is done now; was it wrong then? Is it right now? He has no standard to judge by, since he took to picking holes in the Bible. That is the real reason why we are always seeing the old question discussed, though by now we are thoroughly bored with it, whether our age is degenerate or not. The older generation has a standard of what is done which differs from that of the younger generation. And when the younger generation says, "Ah, but you were just as much a rebel in the eighteen-nineties," the older generation, if it had any sense, would reply, "Yes, and you will be just as much of a stick-in-the-mud in the nineteen-seventies." You must have fixed standards if you are to discuss these things, and they have none; I mean, the great bulk of more or less Anglican Englishmen has none.

The Catholic reaction to the same tendency is different from either. You cannot call it Puritan, even when it protests against the age; for it distinguishes between the importance of the various issues; it is not clouded by a mist of middle-class tradition, does not mistake indulgence as such for sin. Nor yet does it deserve to be called Victorian, because evidently it does not reflect the fashion of a single century. It is strong in controversy, because it takes its stand on unalterable moral principle; not mere ecclesiastical legislation, but the law written in men's hearts. Only, that does not mean that as Catholics we shall avoid all the bother of argument and find ourselves universally respected. We shall find that people are for ever trying to persuade us that our outlook is mediæval, because we stand apart from the sex-madness of our generation. And it makes us unpopular; people laugh at the Puritan but they do not laugh at the Catholic, they feel they are up against something too hard and too formidable for that. A quite new hatred of the Catholic religion is growing up, has grown up within my own lifetime; a hatred of its strict principles on certain points, which our neighbours, though their own liberty of action is not in the least interfered with, dislike as being a criticism of their own conduct, and a criticism which in their heart of hearts they know to be just.

We Catholics have not only to do our best to keep down our own warring passions and live decent lives, which will often be hard enough in this odd world we have been born into. We have to bear witness to moral principles which the world owned yesterday, and has begun to turn its back on to-day. We have to disapprove of some of the things our neighbours do, without being stuffy about it; we have to be charitable towards our neighbours and make great allowances for them, without falling into the mistake of condoning their low standards and so encouraging them in sin. Two of the most difficult and delicate tasks a man can undertake; and it happens, nowadays, not only to priests, to whom it comes as part of their professional duty, but to ordinary lay people. It will come to you, the first time you are asked to be best man at the wedding of a *divorcé*. So we must know what are the unalterable principles we hold, and why we hold them; we must see straight in a world that is full of moral fog.

XXI

MORALITY AND CONVENTION

I T is the nature of the undergraduate to discuss all things in heaven and earth with the utmost seriousness and sometimes with very slight information. And I suppose that those interminable conversations which go on, year after year, in these venerable buildings don't vary much from year to year in their character. I can imagine that buildings like Mob Quad at Merton or the Cottages at Worcester, if they had feelings to express and voices to express them, would protest that they were horribly bored by now with these ceaseless repetitions. Only I suppose there is a slight alteration, from decade to decade, in the choice of themes and the amount of attention devoted to each. I should say, offhand, that before the 1914–18 war the questions most discussed at Oxford were questions of public interest; we were all going to reform the world, by being Socialists or Christian Socialists or young Tories or missionaries or social workers or Nietzschians or proconsuls or philanthropic millionaires; looking back, I can't say that we seem to have done much in that line. Whereas nowadays I fancy that the subjects which command general attention are more self-centred, and very pardonably so. The modern question is "How am I to live?"—first of all in the eminently practical sense, "How on earth am I going to make a living?" (a question which we never considered twenty years ago), and then in the more philosophical sense,

"By what principles (if any) am I personally going to regulate my life?"

The reason why people ask the question "How am I to live?" in the first sense is, clearly, because there aren't nearly so many jobs going. The reason why they ask the second question is, I suppose, mainly what we call in the newspaper headlines and elsewhere "The Breakdown of Convention." Let us stop for a moment at that phrase, and remember what it means. A convention is a rule which all parties agree to abide by for purposes of convenience. Thus it is a convention in England that you should drive on the left-hand side of the road, and it is a convention in most other countries that you should drive on the right-hand side of the road; that is the sort of convention that doesn't break down, and there are a great many other things that would break down if it did. But that is a convention which exists to protect public safety; another set of conventions exists to protect public morality. For instance, it used to be common in Eastern countries, and it is still the practice in certain Eastern countries, that women should never appear in public without having their faces veiled up to the eyes. Nobody pretended that it was actually immoral for a woman to appear unveiled, but rightly or wrongly it was supposed that it would be a safeguard in the interests of morality.

Now, it's quite certain that a good many conventions of that kind have recently disappeared in our own country, for better or for worse. The institution of the chaperone is an obvious instance; the very name, now, has an old-fashioned ring about it. It would be silly to go into details. And people are very fond of pointing out—it's quite true as far as it goes —that such conventions have in themselves no moral value; indeed, that they have a tendency to make morality hypocritical and unreal. And they go on to talk about "conventional morality," and say (or imply) that everybody would be as bad as everybody else if they weren't so frightened of outraging public standards of respectability.

That, of course, is a lie as it stands, but it has this much truth in it—that people of an unadventurous turn of mind, more especially when they have no strong religious lights to guide them, *are* affected in their conduct, more than they know, by the general standards of respectability in which they grow up. There is such a thing as herd-morality. You notice it especially in a matter like divorce, where social considerations necessarily apply. I suppose there were hundreds of people in society thirty years ago who would have gone into the divorce court without a scruple except for the fear of being cut in polite society—a fear which would be quite unnecessary to-day. But the same principle applies even when there is no question of public stigma. People do manage to keep straight just because there is a strong moral tone in the society around them—a moral tone which makes itself felt in a variety of social conventions. And the danger, of course, is that they should confuse propriety with morality. The danger is that in taking the laws of morality and the conventions of propriety equally for granted, they should assume that the two things stand or fall together. And then, if the proprieties go, the moral principles—for such people—will go too.

Those are the people who are asking nowadays, "Why shouldn't I?" And the obvious answer is, "If you think morality a mere matter of social convention, if you are only concerned to consider what other people will say about you, there's no reason why you shouldn't." Nobody will think very much the worse of such a man nowadays if his irregularities are not too blatant. And if he cannot see that morality means something more than a code of human conventions, there is no more to be done with him. What we have to try and persuade him of is: First, that there are such things as right and wrong. Second, that the art of living, and, if I may so describe it, the fun of living, can be found only in regulating your life according to fixed principles of conduct. Third, that there is one single standard of morality, ideally for all people, and practically for all Christian people. And fourth, that if you are really a Christian, the irksomeness of merely obeying negative rules is exchanged for the positive joy of trying to live so as to please our Lord Jesus Christ.

First, there are such things as right and wrong. Whatever else in our human judgments is merely convention, this at least is a fixed principle, that some courses of action deserve to be rewarded, and others deserve to be punished. That whole notion of reward and punishment, of praise and blame, is an elementary notion, born in us, otherwise it could never have got into us. Every attempt to explain away our moral judgments as merely æsthetic or merely utilitarian has completely broken down. It's quite possible to mistake a wrong action for a right one, like the man who assassinates a tyrant. It is quite possible to mistake a right action for a wrong one, like the people who think it is wicked to fight for your country even in a just quarrel. But if right and wrong didn't exist, it would have been quite impossible for such a mistake to arise as to suppose that they did. The human mind has no creative power to have invented for itself such phantasies.

Second, the art of living depends upon living by a rule of conduct, and it is that, really, which lends zest and interest to the performance. Of course, it's true that we've got to make a living, and that struggle lends a certain zest and interest to life; but so far we are no better off than the beasts—they too must struggle for their daily food. But Man, as an intellectual creature, is meant to have a fuller life than this; he has a character to form of which, under God, he is the architect. And any form of art demands rules that you are to work by, laws of harmony, laws of proportion, and so on. To be the artist of his own character, Man must have laws, outside of himself and higher than himself, to which he is to conform his operations. You may go further than that, and say that all art demands an ideal, an ideal which the artist wishes to translate into reality. A man, then, must have ideals to live by; he must want to translate those ideals into reality in his own character. Generally speaking, he has some hero whom he imitates, to whose character he would like to assimilate his own. And the Christian sets before himself the highest of all ideals of character, to imitate as far as possible the life of our Lord Jesus Christ. *He* is the Hero, the Model, whose lineaments we want to translate, with however faltering a hand, on to the canvas of our own lives. A man who is entirely unmoral, if such a creature could exist, would be one who has never tasted life at all.

Next, this law of conduct is the same ideally for all mankind. People talk sometimes about the difference between heathen and Christian morality, and wonder whether perhaps pagan morality wasn't a finer thing. But, of course, in their broad outlines there *is* no difference between Christian and pagan morality at all. The Christian Church didn't suddenly impose on the world a set of moral sentiments of which it had never heard before, a set of moral sentiments with which it violently disagreed. How could Christianity have spread so suddenly and so easily if it had not found a response in the consciences of those to whom it was preached? No, the pagans knew well enough what was right in theory, valued fidelity in married people, continence in young people, even virginity as a form of self-devotion; they knew it was wrong to lie and steal and quarrel and all the rest of it, just as we do. It is possible, of course, for the human conscience to grow blunted, it is possible, therefore, for false standards of morals to prevail, for people to get wrong ideas about the importance of this virtue or that. But the human conscience does admire virtue when it sees it. It can get the values of things wrong, but it doesn't hate good or admire evil for its own sake.

Only, when all that's said and done, the human conscience is such a wavering and uncertain instrument that it does *as a matter of fact* need a code of morals, guaranteed by a supernatural revelation, if it is to keep its true direction. That's not a dogma; it's an ordinary fact of experience. I don't mean that the individual necessarily needs a religion to make him lead a decent life; but the effect upon society of a decline in religion is always a decline in moral standards. And that is why, as I'm always telling you, other people up here are secretly envying you, try and drag you into the conversation when they talk about such things—at the back of their minds they wish that they had your certainty to form the background of their lives.

XXII

CUTTING THE KNOT

"THE Catholic Church forbids divorce"—so we are always reading in the newspapers. Of course, that isn't true. It isn't the Catholic Church which forbids divorce; Almighty God forbids divorce, and all the Catholic Church does is to say she's very sorry, but there it is; the Divine Law will not allow a marriage to be dissolved, so she is afraid she can't very well do anything about it. If it was the Church that had made this law, she would be able to dispense people from this law; the whole point of the situation is that the Church is powerless; she can do nothing. She can no more prevent a person who has two wives being in mortal sin than she can prevent a person who falls off a precipice breaking his neck. It is not part of her *legislation* that a married man should not remarry. It is part of her doctrine that a married man cannot remarry, so long as his first wife is alive. If he goes through the form of marriage, it is an empty farce. Now, let's see what grounds we have for saying that; let us examine it on the three usual grounds of Scripture, of ecclesiastical tradition, and of human common-sense.

We know from Scripture, not merely that our Lord taught the indissolubility of marriage, but that he taught this as part of the natural law. In the beginning it was not so; Moses, for the hardness of their heart, allowed the Jews to divorce their wives in certain aggravated circumstances—that means, in all probability, that the Mosaic law allowed the Jews to divorce their wives for fear that if they weren't allowed to divorce them they would strangle them. How it was exactly that this special dispensation was allowed to the Jews we don't know, all we know is that it was a special dispensation, and one which has now been abrogated by our Lord himself. In the beginning it was not so; God made human kind male and female; he intended that a man should leave father and mother and cleave to his wife. In all sorts of primitive societies all sorts of marriage customs have prevailed; there have been societies in which men had a plurality of wives, in which women had a plurality of husbands; but all that was a degradation, a deviation from the natural law; by his nature, man is monogamous. And it's no good saying that this is unscientific, because the other animals aren't monogamous; that parallel doesn't hold. For one thing, the institution of the family is natural to man, and the institution of the family would become impossible if every man took a fresh wife each spring. For another thing, man is an intellectual creature, and therefore it is foolish to expect that he would be content to live by laws of mere casual instinct. For another thing it is absurd to allow free love unless you also allow free hate; if men are to be allowed to fall in love right and left as the beasts do, then men must be allowed to kill one another right and left, as the beasts do. A civilized society must of necessity have *some* settled principles of marriage; and the principle at which all such societies aim, although they don't always achieve the aim perfectly by any means, is the principle of monogamy.

Even if that weren't so, even if mankind before the Incarnation had been left without any moral principles in the matter, it would still remain true that for us Christian people marriage is a bond which cannot be dissolved, because our Divine Lord has positively laid it down that this should be so.

Once in St Mark and once in St Luke, in a deliberate answer made to the Pharisees who were questioning him upon this precise point, our Lord says quite roundly that the man who puts away his wife and marries another is guilty of adultery. Now, it's quite true that there are two parallel passages in St Matthew where our Lord seems to say that a man may put away his wife on the ground of her misconduct, and in one of those two passages he even seems to imply that in such circumstances a man may remarry. That's quite true, but it doesn't alter the situation. If you take the Protestant higher critical point of view, and say that St Matthew here is in contradiction with the other two Evangelists, then you must prefer their authority to his. For, on the Protestant higher critical reckoning, St Matthew is later than St Mark, and where the two differ, St Mark's account is the original account. There is something splendidly unselfconscious about a man who says (as an Anglican divine said the other day) that in every other part of the Gospel we must prefer St Mark to St Matthew, but just here, just because it happens to suit our book, we must prefer St Matthew to St Mark. As Catholics, of course we have to admit that the discrepancy between the Evangelists is only apparent, and there are so many differences of reading, and of possible rendering, in the passage, that the sense of St Matthew and St Mark can be harmonized in more ways than one without doing any violence to the principles of criticism.

As a matter of fact, we have independent evidence of Christian practice in the matter which is possibly older than any of the Gospels—I mean St Paul's reference in his first epistle to the Corinthians. "But to those who are married it is not I that speak, but the Lord, that a woman should not separate from her husband (or if she does so she must remain unmarried till she is reconciled to her husband), and that a man should not put away his wife." This, then, was how the

7*

earliest apostles understood our Lord's words; there was no exception made in view of marital misconduct. And elsewhere, in writing to the Ephesians, St Paul gives the reason for this attitude of the New Dispensation towards matrimony. Marriage, he says, is a *musterion*, a Sacrament; it is the type of the union between Christ and his Church. Christian marriage, then, must be the mirror of the indissoluble bond which unites the one Christ and his one Church.

And this has been the practice of the Church ever since. One or two local synods in the dark ages tried to make exceptions in favour of the wronged husband or the wronged wife, but such local legislation was always repudiated by the Church, and her stricter standard enforced. She has always permitted judicial separation, on sufficient grounds, but such separation does not make it possible for either party to re-marry. The principle holds good that *a valid and consummated Christian marriage is a bond that binds till death*. I say a Christian marriage, because St Paul himself in the passage I quoted allows the newly converted husband or wife of a heathen to separate and even to remarry, if there is danger to the faith of the Christian party as the result of fidelity to the bond. Theologians dispute as to the grounds on which this extraordinary privilege was conceded. It was conceded, in any case, only to those who had been married as unbaptized heathens, in times of bitter persecution, and to-day it is scarcely heard of. I say a consummated marriage, because it is in the power of the Holy See to dissolve a marriage if as a matter of fact the two parties have never lived together as man and wife. And I say a valid marriage, because if it can be proved legally that the marriage was invalid from the beginning owing to some flaw in the proceedings, then the obligation, which was only an imaginary obligation, naturally ceases.

Every now and then there is trouble over this business I have just mentioned, as there was the other day. What we have to explain to our Protestant friends is this, that a decree of nullity is not the dissolution of a marriage, it is the legal assertion that there has never been any marriage at all. Let me illustrate that difference. Suppose I'm playing patience; I sometimes do. Suppose the game is going badly, and I shuffle the cards and start again—that isn't playing the game; that's like divorce. But suppose I find that five, six, seven and eight of the same suit come out one after another—then I say to myself, "These cards haven't been shuffled properly, I must reshuffle and start again"—that's fair enough, that's like the decree of nullity. I'm not altering the conditions of the problem, I'm only stating that the conditions of the problem were wrong from the start. Of course, our enemies will always say that the Catholic Church uses decrees of nullity as a convenient substitute for divorce, especially where rich people are concerned. That is a cowardly libel. I say a libel, because it's both untrue and damaging; I say cowardly, because it's directed at an institution which cannot sue them for libel. It's quite easy, as a matter of fact, to give instances of poor people who have succeeded in getting a decree of nullity, and instances of rich and powerful people who have tried to get a decree of nullity and failed.

We Catholics, then, are people who don't recognize the possibility of divorce, in the sense in which that word is ordinarily used, living in a world which is beginning to have standards quite different from ours. People with no religion in particular think divorce quite as natural a thing as marriage; even Christians outside the Church are in two minds about it all. Now, apart from tradition, which is the *sensible* view, ours or theirs?

The point we've got to make them realize is this, that whereas Christian marriage, whatever else it is, is a principle, divorce isn't a principle at all, it's only a frantic expedient, a desperate compromise. If all marriages were terminable on either side after five years, or ten years, then that would be an intelligible principle, though I fancy it would lead to a good deal of trouble. Or if we treated marriage merely as a matter of legal partnership, and either side could buy themselves out whenever they liked for a good substantial sum of money, that would be an intelligible principle. But you see we don't do that. We all rally round and sing hymns about the Voice that breathed o'er Eden, and the bride and bridegroom solemnly swear that nothing except death is going to part them, and there are wedding-bells and orange-blossom and old shoes and all the rest of it, and the bride has her married initials stamped on all her wedding presents, and then—then five years afterwards we come to the conclusion that we made a mistake about it, and the two soul-mates weren't soul-mates after all, and the things have to go back to the shop to have fresh initials engraved on them. That's because we're so incurably sentimental, we English. We like to revel in the sentiment of marriage—for better, for worse, for richer, for poorer, in sickness and in health, and so on; but when it comes to the point we find that we don't want our own phrases to mean anything. When Rossetti's wife died, he stood at the graveside and flung the MS. of his unpublished poems into it. Later on, when he was hard up, he dug them up and published them. That's what I call sentimentalism. You do something irrevocable, and then revoke it.

You see, it's all very well to have exceptional legislation for exceptional cases as long as you can make sure that the number of cases is limited. But if you grant legal divorce on grounds of marital infidelity it means, in the first place, that you set a premium on marital infidelity itself; it means, in the second place, that people who are merely bored with one another will be tempted to commit (or to pretend they have committed) offences against fidelity, in order to get a divorce. And the result is a sort of hybrid society where nobody knows whether marriage is an indissoluble bond or not; where, consequently, the best people suffer from the situation, and the worst take advantage of it; where numbers of children are brought up without proper parental control; where the sacramental character of marriage, and even the institution itself, is being brought into such contempt that some people are prepared to think we would be better without it, and are prepared to act on that belief. And all this, of course, is only just starting.*

I say we're all in a mess; the condition of things in which we live is an interim condition of things, and sooner or later the world has got to make up its mind. It must either throw overboard the principle of Christian marriage altogether, replacing it by some different and less permanent kind of contract, or else it must return to the principle that marriage is indissoluble, in spite of the hardship which that principle sometimes brings to individuals, for the sake of general decency and general order. But while the present inconsistent, sentimental attitude prevails, we Catholics have a very clear duty. We must not give people the impression that Catholics abstain from divorce just as they abstain from eating meat on Fridays, as if it were a piece of tiresome ecclesiastical legislation over which Rome is rather old-fashioned, which affects *us* without affecting our neighbours. It is a law of God, written in man's heart; it is a law of Christ, solemnly promulgated by him to the world. This duty, then, of preserving the sanctity of marriage falls upon every intellectual creature in so far as his conscience is rightly informed; it falls especially upon those who call themselves Christians and profess to live by the rule of Jesus Christ. We aren't therefore to talk, you and I, among our non-Catholic friends as if divorce was a thing which didn't matter except where Catholics are concerned. We aren't to register our votes, you and I, for any

* This was written in 1929.

party or any movement which is pledged to further legislation in the direction of free divorce. And later on, when you've settled down in life and have a household of your own, it will be for you to make certain that, as far as possible, your own social example shall be such as to discourage lax views on the subject. I don't mean that it's possible nowadays to refuse altogether to meet people who have been through the divorce courts; it is too late for open protest of that kind to be effective. But in your own choice of friends and in your own exercise of hospitality you will have, to some small degree, the opportunity of influencing the world around you. And we Catholics, remember, are to be the salt of the world, the leaven of human society. That duty of ours becomes, I think, daily more apparent.

I will add one word more, I hope it is unnecessary. If you marry, whether you marry a Protestant or another Catholic, you will marry as a Catholic, and will be understood to be binding yourself under the marriage obligation in a Catholic sense. The Catholic, therefore, who afterwards attempts to get a divorce from his wife is not only being a traitor to his religion, he is being a traitor to his own honour. For it is understood that, whatever other people may mean by their marriage vows, Catholics understand those vows to be terminable only by death, and accept them in that sense. A girl will confide her own happiness to you with all the more confidence because she feels sure that you, being a Catholic, can never look forward to another marriage as long as she lives. And to disappoint that faith of hers is to add treachery to sacrilege. On the other side, if you do marry a non-Catholic, for heaven's sake make sure that she understands the marriage vow in the same sense in which you understand it; that is mere prudence in your own defence.

XXIII

UNSELFISHNESS IN MARRIAGE

LOVE is essentially the effort to sacrifice yourself, to immolate yourself, to another person. And passion is essentially the effort to sacrifice, to immolate, another person to yourself. The man who finds in beauty only something which he must at all costs possess; who finds in innocence something which must be spoilt and defaced, for him; in modesty, something which must be overcome, that he may score a personal triumph; in infidelity, the opportunity of enriching his own experience with as great a variety as possible of amatory adventure—that man is guilty of passion; he is an egoist from first to last. And there is a corresponding egoism on the part of women, which there is no need to discuss here. Contrariwise, the lover's instinct is to devote himself, to be of service, at whatever cost to his own leisure or his own dignity; nay, to obliterate himself if need be, and pass out of the life of the woman he loves, rather than spoil her happiness or interfere with the highest realization of her character—that is love.

So much difference, you see, a whole world of difference, between two experiences either of which is described, in common parlance, as "falling in love." So much difference between the two attitudes in which a man can lead a woman to the altar. I don't suggest that this difference constitutes the whole morality of the affair. Often enough marriages take place, and are regarded by the outside world as "happy" marriages, which are really spoilt by selfishness on the part of husband or wife; there is no breach of the sixth commandment, and yet two lives are baulked of their fruition by this means. I don't say that selfish passion *necessarily* leads to tragedy in marriage; I only say that there is constant danger of it. And on the other side, so weak are we men, so little right have we to judge one another, that you can certainly point to guilty love affairs, such as incur God's displeasure, in which there is nevertheless unselfish love on both sides, a good quality devoted to a bad end. I don't say that unselfish love always and necessarily protects men and women from sinful actions; I only say that it gives the best hope of such protection. Unselfish love is less likely to give rise to moral delinquency; and if it does, we can dare to hope that God will judge it more mercifully.

Well, all that sounds very flat and obvious, and rather like the advice column in *Home Notes*. But, you know, this question of selfishness does lie at the very root of all our present confusion in social life. You see, I suppose it is true to say that women are naturally more unselfish than men; it is hard to imagine that it could be otherwise, since women have to undergo all the altruistic labour of bringing up children. And I think you can say that there has, before our time, been a constant tendency on the part of man to exploit the unselfishness of woman. In all legislation, in all our social judgments, it is quite true to say that the scales have been weighted in favour of our sex. What was sauce for goose hasn't been sauce for gander, in our common, worldly estimation—in Christian morals the parity of position has always been recognized. And not only has there been a tendency to condone the man who is loose in his relations with women outside of wedlock, but in marriage itself men have always been, and still are, too ready to treat their wives selfishly, unfeelingly, inconsiderately, in all the delicate relations of the married state. Men have expected their wives to be echoes and shadows of themselves, instead of realizing that they have lives of their own to live, personalities of their own to express. I wish any of you ever read Meredith's book, *The Egoist*. It is not much read nowadays, because it is full of thought, and people don't like to be made to think when they read novels, they like to have the thinking done for them. It's a profound psychological study of how egoism can kill a romance, what frantic efforts it will make to reconstruct that romance, and, when it fails to do that, how nearly it can succeed in replacing romance by married bondage. If I were dictator, I think I would make it illegal for any young man of decent education to marry until he had not only read *The Egoist*, but passed an examination in it.

Unfortunately, men either didn't read *The Egoist* or didn't assimilate its lessons, but women did. And the revolt of woman, which has been going on all this century, is not a mere political affair, as we try to persuade ourselves that it has been; it's not a mere matter of getting the vote or getting the right to take degrees and practise at the bar and so on. Nor is it a matter of social conventions merely, getting rid of the chaperone and wearing short hair and short skirts, and playing men's games and smoking. It's something far deeper and more significant than that. Beneath the surface of it all there has been a steady revolt on woman's part against the code which made it her business to be professionally unselfish, and so play up, continually, to the selfishness of man. You will recognize from what I said just now that I think women had, in the first instance, the right on their side. But, you know, they are getting their own back with a vengeance. On a privileged occasion like this it is possible to be frank, and to say that many women and many of those especially who try to conform to a modern type, have not been content merely to protest against man's selfishness; they have imitated it. It isn't that they smoke, or swear, or drink cocktails, that isn't the trouble; the trouble is that they are expecting men to do the lion's share in the way of unselfishness; and that doesn't work. Men aren't made that way. That's the cause of half the trouble, at least, which we have been discussing this term.

Well, you will see that I am not being very encouraging to you about your matrimonial prospects. I am inviting you to realize that, unless you marry a type of woman who is not too common nowadays, and is not, nowadays, sought in marriage, *you* have got to be more unselfish men than your fathers and grandfathers were before you; or else there will be shipwreck. And what makes matters worse is that your particular generation is, by force of circumstances, a selfish generation. I am not going to try and bring home that charge of selfishness to you personally; that might look as if I were merely venting a private grievance of my own, and this is no place for such an exercise. I am content to point out that your generation has every temptation to be selfish, every excuse for selfishness, if you like to call it so; and that, just at the moment when it is important for you to be more unselfish than ever. In the first place, you were all brought up as young children during the war.* That was a time, believe it or not, when the greater part of Europe was being unselfish, under the strain of a great emergency. And whatever qualities parents do or do not hand on to their children, one thing is certain; an unselfish parent doesn't make an unselfish child. The unselfish parent, unless the unselfishness is tempered by a rare degree of prudence, indulges the child, does everything for it, is constantly at its beck and call, condones faults, smoothes over difficulties, and, as a general rule, spoils the child. Now, you were brought up by your mothers, not by

* This was written in 1932.

your fathers. Your fathers were fighting, or overworking themselves, or risking their lives somehow; and your mothers were left at home to lavish on you all the care they would have liked to bestow on their husbands—your mothers, you see, still belonged to the unselfish tradition of womanhood. Nothing seemed too good for you, who had come into the world to replace the generation that was fighting and dying. You had rarity value, and you were spoilt.

And then, beset with the temptation to selfishness through passing your nursery days in the time of the Great War, you are beset with a further temptation to selfishness, growing to manhood as you are at the time of the great slump. The question, how you are ever going to get a job, how that job is going to keep you, still worse, how it is going to keep a wife and family, absorbs you as it never absorbed your predecessors. Human nature after all is constant, and the man who is under the immediate necessity of looking after himself has less time, less inclination, to look after other people. He has less scope for unselfish ambition because, on merely economic grounds, his selfish ambitions have to come first. Also, the less prospect there is of having fun during the rest of your lives, the more determined you are, naturally, to have fun while the going is still good. Where are we going to get the unselfish husbands for the women who have come to despise feminine unselfishness, and stamp it as Victorian?

Of all virtues, unselfishness is perhaps the most evidently Christian. It is starred all over the New Testament in phrases which rise familiarly to the lips of the most ignorant; he who loves his life shall lose it, greater love hath no man than this, if any man will come after me, let him deny himself and take up his cross, and so on. A Christian virtue: there is no Latin for selfish and unselfish. There is no Greek for selfish and un-selfish. Unselfishness at its highest point belongs, no doubt, to the more remote paths of holiness; unselfishness of some kind is expected of every Christian; it is, or at least it is meant to be, the badge of our tribe.

And of all failings, selfishness is the most difficult to detect in our own characters. That goes without saying; it is one of the first effects of selfishness to make us feel thoroughly pleased with ourselves. I think occasionally we can detect it in ourselves if we watch, carefully, our judgments of other people. If, for example, you never notice whether other people are selfish or not, that probably means you are selfish yourself, and have lost all sense of the considerateness which human beings ought to show to one another. On the other hand, if you are constantly finding everybody else selfish, that means you are selfish yourself, just as the man who thinks the rest of the world mad may be quite certain that he is a lunatic. If you are continually grousing and discontented, that is again a sure sign. But, of course, selfishness is a thing we should all be on our guard against, whether we are conscious of it or not, for it is close to the roots of all our characters; whether it is in small things, as, for instance, in refusing to play with your young brothers and sisters, or in larger things, like consistently wasting your time and your money when your parents are making sacrifices to give you a university education, you will be pretty sure to find it in your character, if you are unselfish enough to look.

Unselfishness is the best condition of happiness in marriage. That is true, even if the marriage is a childless one; perhaps I ought rather to say, that is especially true if the marriage is a childless one. For a married couple, in those circumstances, are living on their capital; there is no romance of parenthood to complement, to succeed if need be and even to supersede the romance of marriage itself. Marriage, with or without children, can only be what it is meant to be, a lifelong romance, on one condition—that the husband's attitude is one of lifelong courtship. To suppose that, once a woman has said

"Yes," her will thenceforth is entirely her husband's will, so that he can treat her as he likes and dispose of her as he likes, is a supposition which barely works out even in those backward civilizations where women are accustomed to being treated as chattels. In the European civilization of yesterday, that supposition led to a great deal of misery among women, from which they had no legitimate escape. In the civilization of to-day, it leads in a straight line to the divorce court. The women you are going to propose to are less yielding, less compliant, if the bare truth must be told, less unselfish than their mothers, much less so than their grandmothers. And, when courtship is over, when the honeymoon is over, they will still want from you the attentions, the consideration, the readiness to consult their own moods and their own wishes, which will come natural to you during the courtship, during the honeymoon—but not afterwards. That is where you will have to put force on yourself, sometimes, if you are to treat the sacrament of marriage unselfishly. "Giving honour to the female, as to the weaker vessel"—that is how St Peter (who was himself a married man, as the Anglican wedding service rather ungenerously points out) describes the attitude of the Christian husband. Consideration of the wife—that is true especially where the inner sanctities of marriage are concerned; it is true also of the ordinary details of everyday life. The unselfishness, nowadays, has got to come in great measure from your side. If I was giving a conference at Cherwell Edge, I should be putting another side of the case as well; but for you here that's the important thing to understand—don't judge of your wives from your mothers; they belong to a different generation.

And of course, when the question of bringing up a family comes in, you won't need to be reminded that unselfishness is a quality absolutely necessary to Christian parenthood; more so than ever now, when the class to which most of you belong by birth is a class which tends, from one generation to another, to become poorer. You must have noticed, living as you do in a society which discusses its future married arrangements with a singular lack of reticence, how people always try to make it appear as if it was just the other way—as if it was entirely from unselfishness that they don't want to have a family, or don't want to have a large family. "I'm not going to marry till I'm forty," they say, "or anyhow I'm not going to have any children till I'm forty, because if I did I shouldn't have enough money to give them the same educational advantages I've had myself." We must no longer talk of selfish bachelors, as our fathers did; the bachelors are the unselfish people who want to spare several unborn souls the misery of not being brought up at Harrow. I'm afraid, you know, that that kind of unselfishness doesn't really bear looking into. What the man means, at the back of his mind, is that he would rather be known as the father of one son at Harrow than as the father of two sons at Leatherhead. If he were really thinking of the greatest happiness of the greatest number, he would find it difficult to prove that a greater aggregate of happiness is enjoyed by one Harrovian than by two Leatherhead boys. And meanwhile, one would like to ask, what about himself? What kind of car is he going to keep, which club is he going to belong to, where is he going to spend his summer holidays, smoking what kind of cigars? Is he really—that's the point— out to make sacrifices?

Well, I won't pursue that subject, which is rather an ungracious one. What I am concerned to point out is, that the vocation to marriage is also, if it be God's will for you, a vocation to fatherhood. And a vocation to fatherhood is, at the best of times, a vocation which demands unselfishness, and demands a considerable degree of trust in Providence. In having children, you are tying up a great part of your happiness in a set of other human beings who will, sooner or later, escape from your control, and may easily become any sort of nuisance. The man who has a small family does not escape that danger; if anything, he rather increases it; for the children of small families are very apt to be spoilt, and a small family makes no provision for losses by death, by separation, or by disgrace. In common experience, how often one sees that one child can be more of a worry to its parents than six would be! If you scheme for your own happiness in marriage, ten to one you will be disappointed, and you will have the irritating feeling that there is nobody but yourself to blame for it. If you enter upon marriage in a spirit of trust in God's Providence, you are more likely to make a success of it, and if you don't, you will at least be able to see God's plan for you, not God's plan marred by your own interference. Please don't think that I am encouraging all of you to embark upon matrimony at once with no money and no prospects. You must exercise reasonable prudence, or you will be a drag upon others, your own parents particularly. But if and when you are called to that state, you are called to an adventure, and to an adventure which demands generosity—that is the point.

XXIV

THE TORCH HANDED ON

THIS conference is supposed to be about the apostolicity of the Church and I'm rather glad to be doing it myself, because if you put on a visiting preacher to do it he is a tiny bit apt to confuse the issues. Visiting preachers usually start out with the idea that what these young chaps really want is not so much apologetics as good sound moral advice; and the word "apostolic" seems a capital text to start from. It is an excellent thing that every Christian should be an apostle, but the apostolicity of the Church has nothing whatever to do with that. I think you might, as a matter of fact, make out that there is a fifth mark of the Church, which perhaps we might call apostolicality. The Church has at all times had the instinct that if there are heathen or heretics about it is her job to try and convert them as much as the circumstances allow; not to shrug her shoulders and say, "These unfortunate people have a very different world-picture from ours." And that distinguishes her. So I think you could make out a case for the idea that one mark of the true Church is that itch to make converts, which is always described by our non-Catholic neighbours as proselytism, except when they are doing it themselves.

But apostolicity means something quite different. It means being in a position to trace your history, by a continuous tradition, back to the apostles. I say by a continuous tradition, because, of course, in a general way every Christian denomination can trace its history back to the apostles. The Quakers, for example, go back to George Fox in the early part of the seventeenth century; and, of course, George Fox didn't have to invent Christianity himself, he'd learned it from other people, and those other people had learned it from other people, and those other people had learned it from Catholics. But the point is that George Fox deliberately broke away from the main current of Christian tradition, and regarded the Anglican churches as temples of Baal, and the Anglican clergymen as priests of Baal. So that Quaker history doesn't date from the apostles, and doesn't pretend to date from the apostles, it dates from George Fox. Whereas we Catholics do not trace our history back to Edmund Campion at the end of the sixteenth century or to St Augustine of Canterbury at the end of the sixth century; we trace it back to the apostles themselves, to whom our Lord's promises were made, and we wouldn't claim to be the inheritors of those promises unless we could show that we are the heirs of the apostles.

This idea of a continuous spiritual history involves several different claims. In the first place, the whole notion of sacramental life as we understand it demands that certain supernatural powers should be handed on from one generation of Christians to the next; as really, as surely, as certain bodily characteristics are handed down from father to son, generation after generation, in the natural order. The sacramental process by which this tradition is assured has always included, and is often described as, the laying on of hands. We know that the apostles regularly laid hands on those whom they appointed to succeed them in their ministry, and it is a plain matter of history that that process of laying hands on people has been going on ever since. It is only because he is ordained by a bishop that a priest has the power to say Mass and to perform certain other sacraments validly. The word validly means, that a person not so ordained may go through all the motions of performing those sacraments, but when he does nothing happens.

If that were all that was meant by apostolicity, apostolicity would not be a distinctive mark of the true Church. For there are Christian bodies which have a valid ministry and valid sacraments, and yet do not belong to the true Church; most of the Christians in the Near East, whether their doctrines are orthodox or heretical in the light of the early Councils, are in that position; so are the Old Catholics in Holland and elsewhere, a very small body of people who broke away at the time when Infallibility was defined. And, of course, the Anglicans think they have valid orders; and for that matter some of the Presbyterians think they have valid orders; but to go into all that would be a long business, and as we shall see immediately it does not matter a great deal whether they have valid orders or not. For it is possible to have valid orders coming down from the apostles, and yet not to have a continuous spiritual history coming down from the apostles.

How is that? Because a continuous spiritual history means, not merely deriving certain supernatural powers from that fountain of grace which was committed to the apostles, but by deriving from that same apostolical tradition the *right* to minister in God's Church, and to minister in this or that part of God's Church. Our Lord said to his disciples, "As my Father hath sent me, even so send I you"; he commissioned them to act in his name, and this commission to act is something which you must derive by legitimate descent from them, no less than the power to perform spiritual acts. Ever since our Lord said that, the Church has been sending people, commissioning them to minister in this or that place, in this or that capacity, and to minister without her commission is an act of schism. Put it in this way for the sake of clearness;

when you come and make your confession to me here, I can give you absolution. But if you made your confession to me on Boar's Hill, I couldn't give you absolution. Why is that? Because I hold faculties from the Archbishop of Birmingham to hear confessions in his diocese, which is north of the Thames, but Boar's Hill, which is south of the Thames, is in the diocese of Portsmouth, in which, it so happens, I don't hold faculties. On your death-bed, you can get absolution from any priest, even from a Greek Orthodox priest who is in schism, even from a Nestorian priest who is a heretic; because in the hour of death the Church supplies faculties to all priests who have been validly ordained. But for ordinary purposes you must hold a commission from a bishop who is in communion with the Holy See before you presume to exercise any ministerial functions at all.

Our submission is, then, that whenever there has been a schism in the history of Christendom one side was in the wrong, not merely because it broke away from that Catholic, world-wide unity which the true Church must possess, but because it tried to go back upon that apostolic, age-old continuity by which the true Church is equally marked. If you look at the schism which has most to do with controversies which affect our own country, the English Reformation, you can see at once that it was a schism between the supporters of an old, continuous tradition, and the supporters of a new order of things. I know that Anglican controversialists eagerly maintain the contrary; try to make out that the continuous tradition lies with them, not with us. But the tradition of Anglicanism does not go back to those thirteen or fourteen bishops who were left over at the end of Queen Mary's reign. It goes back to the new set of bishops, whether validly consecrated or not it doesn't matter, whom Queen Elizabeth intruded into their sees, without any ecclesiastical authority for doing so. It is from them, from Queen Elizabeth's nominees, that the Anglican Church of to-day derives, in the last resort, its commission.

Further, in order to be apostolic a Church must have continuity, not only of life but of faith. People sometimes accuse us Catholics of having added to the faith; of having foisted in doctrines which were no part of the original deposit, that of the Immaculate Conception, for example. But nobody seriously accuses us of having subtracted from the faith; of having dropped any article of belief which was an integral part of theology as theology was understood by the early Fathers. And that's important. The apostles, you see, were in the first instance witnesses; people who could bear testimony to certain things they had seen and heard, and hand on that testimony to those who came after them. Every Catholic bishop is the repository of a tradition which he took over from his predecessor and is bound to hand on, un-diminished, to his successor. That's why, if he has time and opportunity, a Catholic bishop on his death-bed calls his canons together and makes a solemn profession of faith; he wants to make it clear that, in his time at least, the deposit of tradition has not been tampered with.

Continuity of life, continuity of faith—there you have the essentials of that mark of apostolicity by which we distinguish the true Church. I always feel we should do well to include another kind of continuity, which is not often mentioned in this connection, what you may call continuity of type. The Catholic type, that's a thing which doesn't change with the centuries. You could say a lot about it; you could write a book about it; but the obvious, salient point to raise about it is this, that it is tenacious, has a firm grip on the old things and is suspicious of novelties. Quite often it pushes this tendency too far, and has to admit that there was something in the new things after all. It is a rather amusing and a very salutary reflection that St Thomas was regarded as a dangerous innovator because he wanted to interpret Christian theology in terms of Aristotle. "Good old Plato," people said, "what's wrong with Plato? He was good enough for St Augustine, and he ought to be good enough for us." Well, of course, they were wrong; and yet in a sense they were right; their instinct was right. At the time, no doubt, the thing looked like some sort of ramp. We've all suffered from it, this Catholic instinct of caution; God knows I have. But, though it has the defects of its qualities, the Catholic type is admirably adapted to secure, what its first business is to secure, the permanence on earth of a great religious tradition, whose content is of the supernatural, and whose origins are divine.

If for a moment I may assume the airs of a bishop on his death-bed, and throw back my regard over the past, I would say that this instinct of tenacity marks us off, us Catholics, from all that I have known of non-Catholic religion in Oxford, since I knew Oxford. As a member of this University, I have the age of Christ; it is thirty-three years since I matriculated. During the first nine of those years, I knew Oxford as a Protestant; during the last thirteen as a Catholic; and during all that time, the modern religious debate has been constantly the subject uppermost in my thoughts. I can remember, when I was an undergraduate, a sermon from the Bishop of London, I mean the one who is just retiring, then at the height of his remarkable influence. He preached about the faith, and gave us a parable, probably from some incident in the South African War, about a wounded soldier with a flag in his hands, "slipping . . . slipping." And then, of course, he told us that we mustn't let the faith slip like that. But I'm afraid it is what we were doing, and what those who followed us have been doing ever since. The instinct of holding on to a religious tradition which you have received, handing it on undiminished to others, where is it now, outside the Catholic Church? I don't say that there aren't many excellent

Christians among our non-Catholic friends; of course there are; many of them make us feel ashamed of ourselves. But take a mass observation of our contemporaries, and you will see, or at least I think I see, the traditions we held, the assumptions with which we faced life, thirty years ago, slipping between their hands.

It is just over forty years ago now, that Leo XIII first allowed Catholics to go up to Oxford and Cambridge. If he had foreseen the course of things, he would have said to them, "I send you forth as lambs in the midst of wolves." Wolves in sheep's clothing if you like; wolves in Old Etonian ties and so on, but wolves for all that; I mean, in the sense that their bewildered acquiescence in our modern materialism is an influence working for the labefactation of all sane principles. If he had seen you sitting here now, that great Pope would have wished you, I think, the gift of tenacity.

Forty years, and now the Oxford chaplaincy is to change hands for the fifth time.

Remember this—the chaplaincy is not like a parish, in which most of the work is routine work, and everything goes on very much the same, as Father Smith succeeds Canon Jones. The chaplain's work is a series of frantic experiments made in the dark, based almost entirely on personal contact. That means that every chaplain has to work in his own way, tackle the situations that arise in the fashion which is best suited to his own individual gifts, his own individual tastes. I am leaving to my successor a document about six times as long as this sermon, explaining to him exactly how everything has been run while I have been here. I have left it to him in the certainty, and almost in the hope, that he will set to work on perfectly different lines as soon as he finds his feet here. He will probably want to do all sorts of things which I have never done. And that will arouse, in those of you who are left here next year, that spirit of tenacity which, as I have been suggesting to you, is suspicious of every change, which treats every fad of the last incumbent as if it were part of the deposit of faith. It never used to be done like that (you will find yourself saying) in the old days.

What I want to say to you, while I have still the opportunity of registering my protest, is, "For heaven's sake don't say that." That habit of canonizing the last man, gracious in itself, leads to such a lot of petty and unnecessary friction. I want you to treat my successor as the chaplain whom God has sent you, and to make things easy for him, as far as possible, at the start; after that, you won't need any encouragement from me. But just at the start, do try to make things easy for him. Go and see him, and let him make your acquaintance, as soon as he has had time to comb out the freshers; don't hang about waiting for an invitation to dinner. I remember so well, you see, how difficult it was starting on this job. Don't all go rushing off to other churches in the town, as some of you do already, just because a new man won't be able to see whether you come or not.

I've been speaking to those who will still be up next year; perhaps at unnecessary length—after all, the work of a University chaplain is written in water; even as he speaks, the moving finger writes. My predecessor, a man of mature wisdom, was once talking to me about some innovation he had introduced; and I said, "But wasn't that unpopular?" To which he replied, "Very; but then, an undergraduate only lasts three years." Let me speak to you for a moment not as the undergraduates you are, but as the Catholic laymen in the world you soon will be. One point I have tried to urge on you at the end of each summer term and now let me leave it with you as my testament. Every one of you, when he goes down, ought *somehow* to enter into the corporate life of the Catholic body; not just to be the kind of Catholic who is seen slinking off to Mass every Sunday, at the Oratory or at the

Cathedral, a lost unit in the crowd. If nothing else occurs to you, at least do this—get to know your parish priest, and ask if there isn't any way in which you can be of use to the parish, even if it's only by taking elderly and infirm people to church in your car—how many of you have ever thought of that? You see, a man's religion fits more naturally into the scheme of his life if it involves for him something, however little, over and above the plain duty of saying his prayers.

That is all the parting request I would make, except for myself, that you would pray for me sometimes. God bless you, and make us meet in heaven.